The Heart-Watcher's Cook Book
Low cholesterol cookery

The Heart-Watcher's Cook Book
Low cholesterol cookery

by Cecilia Norman

Foreword by P.L. Humpherson, B.Sc., S.R.D.

Illustrated by Elsa Willson

HIPPOCRENE
BOOKS, INC.

New York, N.Y.

Second impression 1975

© 1975 by Cecilia Norman

All Rights Reserved

Hippocrene Books, Inc.
171 Madison Avenue
New York, N.Y. 10016

Library of Congress Catalog Card Number 74-22846
ISBN 0-88254-319-9

Printed in Great Britain
at the Alden Press, Oxford

Contents

Illustrations

Conversion notes

The weights and measures used in this book are British measures, and the following is a list of such, together with the Metric equivalents for those British measures.

British measures (Imperial)

16 ounces (oz.)	= 1 pound (lb.)	
14 pounds	= 1 stone (st.)	
20 fluid ounces (fl. oz.)	= 1 pint (pt.)	
2 pints	= 1 quart (qt.)	
8 pints	= 1 gallon (gal.)	

NOTE: 1 British fluid ounce = 1 American fluid ounce. Although not used in this book, 1 British cup = $\frac{1}{2}$ pint (10 fl. oz.), and $1\frac{1}{4}$ American cups are approx. equal to 1 British cup.

1 tablespoon (tbsp.)	= 15 millilitres (ml.) = 3 teaspoons
1 teaspoon (tsp.)	= 5 millilitres

Metric equivalents

1 oz.	= 28·35 grammes (g.), which is taken as 30 g.
1 lb.	= 453·6 g. which is taken as 450 g.
1 pint (Imperial)	= 568·2 ml., which is taken as 550 ml.
1 fl. oz.	= 28·4 ml., which is taken as 30 ml.
1 kilogramme	= 2·225 lb.
1 litre	= 1·75 pint (Imperial)

American measures

1 American cup	= 8 fl. oz., $\frac{1}{2}$ American pint or approx. 230 ml.
1 American tbsp.	= $\frac{1}{2}$ fl. oz. or approx. 15 ml.
1 American tsp.	= $\frac{1}{8}$ fl. oz. or approx. 5 ml.
1 American pint	= 16 fl. oz.

NOTE: If the reader is using standard American spoons these can be reckoned as the same size as used in this book. The only real caution that needs to be exercised by an American using these recipes is to remember that $\frac{1}{4}$ pint equals a generous American $\frac{1}{2}$ cup and $\frac{1}{2}$ Imperial pint is almost exactly $1\frac{1}{4}$ cups, $\frac{3}{4}$ pint equals a scant 2 cups and 1 Imperial pint is exactly $2\frac{1}{2}$ American cups.

Foreword

Most people would rather take drugs than alter something that affects life-long habits and tastes. Often a special diet cannot be replaced by drugs and this can affect not only the patient's eating habits but also those of his family and friends. This problem has to be faced by the wife and cook.

To hear that a member of a household has a raised serum cholesterol stimulates worry—however much help has been given at the hospital—and the desire to do the best possible while continuing to feed the family. A housewife is a busy person and she cannot cook separately for the patient. The whole family has to be involved.

This is the situation which faced Cecilia Norman and she could find little published to help her. Being a cookery teacher, keen on writing books that require preliminary research, she set about finding out all she could about a low cholesterol diet. She then experimented on her family and evolved numerous recipes for everyday meals as well as dinner parties. The result is a book containing recipes both interesting and tempting and suitable for all, while helping to produce menus that contain all the nutrients required for health. A section also gives sensible guide lines for eating out.

However, hyperlipidaemia, of which a raised serum cholesterol is a part, is a complex medical problem—a problem which is still being thoroughly investigated while the general public is becoming more aware of it and anxious to try to avoid the consequences.

Whether egg yolks, cheese, nuts, cocoa, olives, liver or

roes are allowed varies, and each patient must consult and follow the advice of the dietitian or doctor who originally explained or prescribed the diet.

London   P. L. Humpherson, B.Sc., S.R.D.

1. What is cholesterol?

It has been established that a cholesterol-controlled diet helps to lower the incidence of coronary thrombosis. There have been at least two dietary experiments which have demonstrated the link between such a diet and a decrease in coronary attacks. If you are concerned about your heart or arteries—or those of anyone else in your household—and provided you are not suffering from low cholesterol or allied ailments, this book should be of great help to you in understanding the problem and providing a number of recipes for your use.

The word cholesterol comes from the Greek 'chole' meaning bile and 'steros' meaning solid. Cholesterol is produced from the food you eat and by synthesis in the body by the liver, and is a fatlike waxy substance. It is found in all animal tissue, but only traces have ever been discovered in foods of vegetable origin. Fat is lighter than water and cholesterol is important in helping carry fat through the liquid bloodstream. Fatty deposits can build up in the blood, coating the arteries and causing them to become narrow. If a clot subsequently forms, it will not pass through the arteries easily and should this happen in an artery close to the heart, a coronary attack is likely to occur.

Two hundred mg. of cholesterol per ml. is a desirable level in the blood and a count in excess of 260 mg. would be considered high. A sensible diet will control the cholesterol level and could help to prolong life. A diet low in cholesterol, that is to say a daily intake of between 300 and 350 mg., is desirable. Fats in food are of paramount importance in determining the quantity of cholesterol in the diet. The total intake of all types of fat should be about one third of the calories in your diet. Thus if you consider 2,700 calories per day to be a normal diet, not more than 900 calories of fat should be ingested. This is not a very great amount as can be seen from Table 2, Calorific Values, on page 206.

When considering fats in the diet, remember you only see two fifths, for the other three fifths are hidden in the remainder of the food. Cutting away the fat from the steak does not mean that you are not consuming any fat at all.

Fats, which in technical data are called 'lipids', contain three types of fatty acid.

1 Saturated—sometimes called stearic.
2 Mono-unsaturated—sometimes called oleic.
3 Poly-unsaturated—known as PUFA but shortened throughout this book to PU.

PU acids are three in number—linoleic, arachidonic and linolenic. Linoleic acid is an essential fatty acid (EFA) and can only be ingested from food for it cannot be made by the body. However, when linoleic acid is absorbed from the diet, the body can then make the second EFA, arachidonic acid. The third PU acid, linolenic, is not an EFA and is not, therefore, a substitute for linoleic acid.

Diets which are completely free of EFAs could cause severe skin diseases to develop, whilst growth could be stunted and reproductive capacity damaged.

PU acids will reduce the level of blood cholesterol and that is why it is so important to know which foods contain this substance and in what quantity. (See Table 3, Fatty Acid Content of Food, page 212.)

It is essential to eat twice as much PU acids as saturated acids. Throughout the book I mention PU margarine and PU oil. Using these in place of saturated margarines and oils will actively lower cholesterol and prevent the arteries from becoming clogged. Saturated acids consist of the largest and heaviest fat molecule, mono-unsaturated acids are slightly smaller fat molecules, and the smallest of all are the PU molecules. A molecule is a chemical combination of two or more atoms to form a specific substance as, for example, a fatty acid.

Butter is excluded from the diet because of its cholesterol

content and will be replaced for 'spreading' by margarine. Some of the margarines manufactured are soft and some are hard. In normal circumstances hard margarine is the most suitable for pastry making, but it should not be used as it is 'hydrogenized'. In the manufacture of hard margarines, hydrogen is pumped through the oils forcing a change in the chemical construction and changing the poly-unsaturates into saturates. PU margarine is easily recognisable by its soft texture, but do be sure to note the composition and buy the margarine that has the highest proportion of linoleic acid.

In cooking, PU oils may be used instead of margarine or unsuitable cooking fats. It is thought that mono-saturated acids (e.g. oleic) are neutral in their effect on cholesterol levels and therefore their use is neither beneficial nor harmful. Olive oil, as can be seen from the table on page 212 has a high oleic acid content, but oils with a higher proportion of linoleic acid should be used if possible. Peanut oil has 85% more linoleic acid than olive oil, whilst corn, soya bean and cotton seed oils have 40% more linoleic acid than peanut oil and the best oil of all from this point of view is safflower oil. Two tablespoons of safflower oil provide the same quantity of linoleic acid as three tablespoons of cornoil. So by using the former you will be saving 125 calories. (See Table 4, Comparison of Saturated and Unsaturated Fatty Acids in Oils and Fats, on page 215.)

The list of contents printed on the labels of canned foods should always be read carefully. Unless a specific 'good' fat or oil is mentioned, it would be better to refrain from the purchase. The term 'vegetable fat' or 'vegetable oil' is not a sufficient indication of fatty acid ratios. Provided one quarter of your calories are taken in PU acids, the cholesterol level will be lowered, the smaller molecules of linoleic acid having a liquefying action and easing the flow of blood through the arteries.

There are several factors held to be contributory to coronary heart disease:

Emotional stress
Heavy cigarette smoking
Lack of exercise
Obesity
Heredity

Those with diabetes, gout, high blood pressure (hyper-cholesterolemia) and men over the age of 40 are the most likely victims. Someone having a single one of these factors will run double the risk of heart disease, and if three or four are applicable the chances will be ten times as great. To minimise the risks as far as possible, the normal healthy person should reduce his smoking, take regular exercise and make sure that he is not overweight.

A calorie is a measurement of energy which is supplied by food for maintaining the body processes. Too many calories will make you fat, but if you are not overweight, you must be careful not to over-slim. Table 5 on page 216 shows the average correct weight adopted by insurance companies when considering life policies. When slimming you should endeavour to cut down the calorie intake to 1,500 per day.

The cholesterol level will lower at the same time as weight reduction occurs, but when your 'target' weight is reached, and you revert to a less strict diet, the cholesterol level will tend to return, although it should not reach the original level. It takes two years on a low cholesterol diet before any lasting effect can result and the risk of a coronary attack is lessened. But this regime is so easy and satisfying that the goal will not be found hard to reach and you should remain happily on the diet indefinitely. (See Table 6, Choice of Foods, on page 218.)

DO control the intake of foods containing cholesterol.
DO eat twice as much unsaturated fats as saturated fats.
DO ensure that one quarter of the daily calories are in PU fats.
DO reduce foods containing saturated fats to the minimum.
DO NOT eat too much.
DO serve fish in lieu of meat twice a week and poultry once a week.
DO use PU margarine and oils in cooking.
DO take regular exercise
DO reduce cigarette smoking.
DO NOT worry.

The recipes that follow in this book are suitable and appetizing for all the members of a family. Those not following the diet may spread butter on their bread, drink whole milk and have their egg for breakfast if they wish.

2. Dietary recommendations and calorie control

It is necessary to provide a balance between an adequate calorie intake and a low cholesterol diet. If there are fourteen main meals to the week these can best be divided as follows:-

PROTEIN FOODS. 6–8 oz. daily (raw weight)

Chicken ⎫
Turkey ⎬ To be the basis for nine meals per week
Veal ⎪
Fish ⎭

Beef ⎫
Lamb ⎬ To be used for not more than five meals per
Pork ⎪ week
Ham ⎭

It should be remembered that the meat should be as lean as possible and the poultry and fish served without skin. Duck and goose are not recommended.

As an alternative to the meat meals, pulses give a protein substitute and as they are vegetable there is no cholesterol content. These include

Lentils
Split peas
Soya protein (obtainable in health food shops as meat substitute with meat flavouring)
Chick peas
Baked beans
Butter beans

EGG YOLKS. Three per week.

Do not forget that this number includes those used in cooking and 'hidden yolks' in commercially prepared foods.

LIVER. Four oz. not more than *once* per week.

Liver is high in cholesterol but rich in iron and vitamins.

This can be used in place of a meat meal, but $3\frac{1}{2}$ oz. of liver has the same cholesterol value as 1 standard egg yolk. Never use pig's liver.

SHELLFISH. Four oz. may be used in place of 1 standard egg yolk occasionally.

Shellfish are high in cholesterol and low in calories.

FISH. When fish are used in a diet to achieve a low calorie, high protein ratio, a selection is needed to obtain low-fat varieties. When fish is intended as a means of regulating cholesterol, both the fat and the PU content of the oil or fat must be considered. The belly flap area of a fish is apt to have a higher fat content than the remainder of the fish as are the red or dark sections. The steaks cut from the tail end have a lower oil content than those from the head end of a fish. Even though fish oils, unlike vegetable oils, sometimes contain as much saturated fatty acids as they do PU acids, the latter are so efficient as cholesterol depressants that they much more than compensate for the presence of saturated fatty acids. Thus fish oils are weight-for-weight several times as effective as vegetable oils.

VEGETABLES AND FRUIT. At least 12 oz. per day.

In addition to this general rule, there should also be an intake of 4 oz. per day of items rich in Vitamin A and 4 oz. rich in Vitamin C.

Vitamin A. Vegetables and fruit (fresh or canned):

Broccoli	Apricots
Cabbage	Gooseberries
Carrots	Mango
Red peppers	Melon
Spinach	
Tomatoes	
Watercress	

These vegetables and fruits contain carotene which the body converts into Vitamin A. However the rate of absorption is poor, and the amount of carotene has to be divided by three to find how much Vitamin A it will form.

Vitamin C. Vegetables and fruit:

Raw cabbage	Black currants
Broccoli	Grapefruit juice (canned)
Kale	Fresh grapefruit
Leeks	Lemons
Lettuce	Melon
Parsley	Orange juice (canned)
Green peppers	Oranges
Raw sprouts	Fresh pineapple
Watercress	Strawberries

It is important to provide 'Vitamin A' vegetable and fruit in the diet because the other normal sources of true Vitamin A e.g. eggs, liver, liver oil, milk, and milk products are limited in the low cholesterol diet. Skimmed milk has only a small Vitamin A content. Vitamin A is stored in the body and therefore the intake required can be calculated over a week and not necessarily on a daily basis. One half pound each of canned carrots, tomatoes, cabbage, spinach and apricots for example in a week when added to the normal PU oil and margarine intake would provide adequate Vitamin A in the diet.

One orange or grapefruit or 1 oz. green peppers or 6 raw brussel sprouts will supply all of Vitamin C needed for a day. Boiling diminishes the value as Vitamin C dissolves in the water. All other fruits are suitable to make up the daily 4 oz. with the exception of olives and avocadoes which are high in fat content and therefore high in calories. Vitamin C is not stored in the body, and therefore must be in the daily diet.

BREADS, CEREALS AND PASTAS. Use at least four servings per day.

Pasta should be made without saturated fat or eggs.

1 slice bread
1 (average-sized) plate cereal and skimmed milk
3 oz. cooked rice
3 oz. cooked macaroni or spaghetti

MILK OR PERMISSIBLE MILK PRODUCTS. Three-quarters to 1 pint per day.

Choose from skimmed milk
                buttermilk (made from skimmed milk)
                yoghurt (low fat)
                cottage cheese

FATS AND OILS. Two to 4 tbsps. per day.

Choose, of course, from PU oils and margarines; 2 tbsps. PU oil = 252 calories. DO NOT LIMIT the intake of PU fats and substitute carbohydrates such as starchy and sweet foods as this will increase the weight and deny the body its vital linoleic acid. It will also probably lower the amount of Vitamin A in the diet.

Repeated use of fat and oil for frying causes various chemical changes. The more often the same fat is reheated the more degraded it becomes. PU fats are more susceptible to degradation than saturated fats; as the fat is used over and over again, the linoleic acid content decreases. So do not use the same fat more often than economy requires. The goals are:

(a) to maintain the proportion of calories as total fat above 35% and as close as possible to 40%
(b) to reduce the proportion of calories as saturated fat to 10% or less;
(c) to increase the proportion of calories as PU fat to 10% or more;
(d) to reduce dietary cholesterol intake to an average of 300/350 mg. per day.

Three hundred and fifty mg. is not a very great amount, but with the recommendations in this chapter, it should not be too difficult to maintain, and will even allow something spare for the odd meal out when the milligrams are more difficult to watch.

Calorie requirements vary according to age, sex and the type of life led. Although it is important not to consume too many calories, it is equally vital not to consume too few. Calories produce energy which is needed by every cell in the body. Muscle cells use energy when they relax and contract during voluntary movement of the limbs and involuntary movement of the heart and digestive system.

Nerve cells use energy to pass impulses between the brain and other tissues to regulate and co-ordinate body functions. Every gland and organ needs energy, which is required to produce new cells and which keeps the body warm.

Three of the nutrients in food, carbohydrate, protein and fat, all produce calories.

1 gram carbohydrate = 4 calories of a type which supply heat and energy

1 gram protein = 4 calories used for body building and repair

1 gram fat = 9 calories which give heat

Although fat is more than twice as 'fattening' as protein and carbohydrate, it is more satisfying and staves off hunger for a comparatively longer time.

Men aged up to 65 require 2,700 to 3,600 calories per day depending on their occupation. The most active man needs the greatest intake. Women need between 2,200 and 2,500. After retirement age the requirement for both sexes lessens: 2,200 for men and 2,000 for women is an approximate guide.

Example day's diet cholesterol content

6 oz. meat (beef)	120 mg.
$\frac{3}{4}$ egg	183 mg.
$\frac{3}{4}$ pint skimmed milk	12 mg.
	315 mg.

Table 1 Cholesterol content of foods

Item	Amount of cholesterol in	
	100 mg. edible portion (mg.)	Edible portion of 1 lb. as purchased (mg.)
Beef, raw:		
with bone	70	270
without bone	70	320
Brains, raw	>2,000	>9,000
Butter	250	1,135
Caviar or fish roe	>300	>1,300

Item	Amount of cholesterol in 100 gm. edible portion (mg.)	Edible portion of 1 lb. as purchased (mg.)
Cheese:		
cheddar	100	455
cottage, creamed	15	70
cream	120	545
other (25% to 30% fat)	85	385
Cheese spread	65	295
Chicken, flesh only, raw	60	—
Crab:		
in shell	125	270
meat only	125	565
Egg white	0	0
Egg yolk:		
fresh	1,500	6,800
frozen	1,280	5,800
dried	2,950	13,380
Fish:		
steak	70	265
fillet	70	320
Heart, raw	150	680
Ice cream	45	205
Kidney, raw	375	1,700
Lamb, raw:		
with bone	70	265
without bone	70	320
Lard and other animal fat	95	430
Liver, raw	300	1,360
Lobster:		
whole	200	235
meat only	200	900
Margarine:		
all vegetable fat	0	0
two-thirds animal fat, one-third vegetable fat	65	295
Milk:		
fluid, whole	11	50
dried, whole	85	385
fluid, skim	3	15

Item	Amount of cholesterol in 100 gm. edible portion (mg.)	Edible portion of 1 lb. as purchased (mg.)
Mutton:		
with bone	65	250
without bone	65	295
Oysters:		
in shell	>200	>90
meat only	>200	>900
Pork:		
with bone	70	260
without bone	70	320
Shrimp:		
in shell	125	390
flesh only	125	565
Sweetbreads	250	1,135
Veal:		
with bone	90	320
without bone	90	410

Note: 100 gm. = 3½ oz. approx.
    1 large egg yolk = 428 mg.

Adapted from Table 4, *Composition of Foods Raw, Processed & Prepared*, Handbook No. 8, U.S. Dept. of Agriculture.

When dining out it can be quite difficult to select suitable foods without embarrassing your friends. If you have time, glance through the selections offered for all the courses, when you will be able to decide on which part of the meal you wish to go comparatively wild. If you do take one of the courses with almost as exotic a choice as your companions, they are much less likely to notice that you are restricting yourself to a diet at all.

For 'starters' it is nearly always possible to have melon or grapefruit. Hors d'oeuvre variés can be eaten by avoiding salami and carefully leaving the yolks of the eggs on the side of the plate. Even a solitary sardine could hardly be said to be a disaster. Consommé without egg garnish is

100% acceptable, fruit juices are fine and the avocado is permissible for the cholesterol level, but highish on calories.

French onion soup is not too bad, but omit thickened soups, prawn cocktails, patés and terrines. Whitebait can be ordered provided the remainder of the meal is to have the strictest care. Naturally avoid butter and take your bread or rolls dry.

For the main course a lean steak at a steak house will weigh about 6 oz. and this only constitutes 140 mg. cholesterol. Cut away all the surplus fat and avoid sauces and put any pats of butter off the steak on to your side plate so it does not melt into the meat. Grilled sole, trout or halibut are permissible but lobster and crab are definitely not. All vegetables can be eaten, but some are served tossed in butter —very often french beans are served this way—and these should be avoided. Even a few french fried can be included.

Choose fruit for dessert, or if there is a baba or savarin, naturally pushing the cream firmly on one side of the plate, these two contain little to increase the cholesterol level even if they may be a little generous in calories for the weight-watchers. Pancakes are usually thin and would add a very small amount to your intake. Jellies and compôtes contain nothing harmful but NEVER eat shortcake, pastries, custard tarts, crème caramel, zabaglione, profiteroles, charlotte russe and gâteaux.

For the cheese course, if you have had a dessert try to avoid it altogether, save perhaps for a dry biscuit. But instead of a sweet, a small piece of cheese, will only give 22½ mg. cholesterol which would be no disaster. You must avoid stilton and full cream cheeses, however.

Finally at the coffee stage, black is best, but dark brown with a little milk makes virtually no difference, but again NO CREAM. As for the brandy or port, there are no rules in this book about alcohol.

General eating habits in other counties seem to have had an effect on the serum cholesterol of their population. In the undernourished countries, deaths mainly occur for other reasons, and rice as a staple diet provides no cholesterol problems whatsoever. At the other end of the scale in affluent societies, particularly American, the incidence is high. This is not due only to a rich diet but also because of hypertension and stress which are contributory factors to the disease, but a penalty of good living. In France there is a higher death rate from alcoholism, so that there are other dangers from food and drink than those merely confined to coronary problems. The Japanese eat a considerable volume of fish, most of it stewed, and make much use of soya sauce. This type of cooking is highly desirable. Certain ethnic groups in Europe, including England, tend to eat a large proportion of rich fattening foods which could form a link with their high early death rate. Provided coconut oil is not used for frying, the English fish and chip shop is playing a very large part in keeping the British healthy.

Almond-crème Soup
4 oz. ground almonds
1½ pints skimmed milk
2 tbsps. cold water
1 tbsp. PU oil
1 tbsp. plain flour
1 tbsp. finely chopped onion
1 tbsp. grated carrot
1 egg yolk
Salt and pepper
Bay leaf

1 Heat the milk with onion, carrot, salt, pepper and bay leaf and leave to infuse 20 min.
2 Blend oil with the flour and a little cold water in a saucepan.
3 Strain the milk infusion onto the mixture and stir well.
4 Add ground almonds and bring to boil.
5 Place saucepan over a slightly smaller pan, one quarter filled with boiling water and cook 20 min.
6 Beat egg yolk with a little cold milk, and add to hot soup, blending carefully.
7 Serve at once garnished with croutons.

If you have a double saucepan or porringer available, use it for this recipe instead of the two saucepans in step 5. One sixth egg yolk per serving.

Asparagus Soup

1 medium sized (12 oz.) can asparagus cuts or tips
2 oz. shredded cooked chicken or turkey
½ pint water
½ pint skimmed milk
1 chicken stock cube (optional)
2 tsps. cornflour

1 Place water and milk in saucepan with cornflour and blend.
2 Add all other ingredients.
3 Bring to boil, adjust seasoning and serve.

This thin soup with chunks of asparagus and chicken shreds has a bland flavour and may precede a poultry or fish dish. A very easy soup to prepare; use up your 'left overs' here.

Beetroot Soup

½ lb. cooked beetroot
1 oz. PU margarine
1 oz. plain flour
1 pint stock
¼ pint skimmed milk
2 tsps. worcestershire sauce
Salt and pepper
Pinch of sugar

1 Peel and dice beetroot.
2 Place margarine, flour and milk in saucepan.
3 Whisk over low heat until mixture boils, thickens and a stiff sauce is formed.
4 Add stock gradually, whisking all the time.
5 Add beetroot, worcestershire sauce, sugar and seasoning.
6 Cover and simmer 20 min.
7 Liquidize or press through a sieve.
8 Adjust seasoning. Serve hot.

Farmhouse Soup

2 tbsps. PU oil
1 lb. shredded mixed vegetables (carrots, onions, celery, leeks, cabbage, parsnips)
2 oz. pearl barley
3 pints water
1 pint skimmed milk
Pinch thyme and pinch rosemary
Salt and pepper
2 tsps. worcestershire sauce

1 Sauté vegetables in oil in large saucepan until soft.
2 Add all other ingredients and season to taste.
3 Cover and simmer for 2 hr, stirring occasionally.

French Onion Soup

4 Large onions
Small clove of garlic
3 tbsps. PU oil
1½ pints beef stock
¼ pint dry white wine
Salt and pepper to taste

1 Peel and slice onions thinly.
2 Melt oil in saucepan. Add onions and crushed garlic and sauté until golden brown.
3 Add stock and wine. Stir well and bring to boiling point.
4 Add salt and pepper, cover and simmer for 10 min.

Traditionally a slice of toasted french bread is put in the soup plate (before the soup) and sprinkled with grated cheese. If you have no home cooked stock, use a can of beef consommé, and make up the total quantity of liquid with water. Should you decide to use beef stock cubes, you must remember that they contain a small quantity of beef fat, and are rather salty.

Onions are easier to peel and slice if first cut in half through stalk to root. Peel the skin back from the stalk end and grasping the root with the flat part of the onion on a board, slice finely, starting furthest away from the fingers.

Gaszpacho

2 lb. ripe tomatoes
1 spanish onion
1 medium sized cucumber
1 crushed clove of garlic
Salt and pepper
¼ pint safflower oil
2 tbsps. red wine vinegar
1 tbsp. sherry
2 green peppers (de-seeded)
Dash of tabasco sauce
Celery salt

1 Cover tomatoes with boiling water, leave for 5 min. and then press through a sieve.
2 Finely chop onion, cucumber and peppers.
3 Combine onion, cucumber and peppers with garlic, salt and pepper.
4 Gradually stir in oil and then add vinegar, sherry and celery salt.
5 Add tomato pulp and then the smallest dash of tabasco sauce.
6 Chill at least 2 hr. Serve with paprika croutons.

Gaszpacho is a delicious piquant summer soup. Almost a vegetarian meal in itself.

To de-seed pepper, cut in half through the stalk. It is then simple to remove most of the seeds with one press of the thumb, the remainder will wash out under cold running water. The seeds must always be removed because of their bitter flavour.

Goulyassuppe

½ lb. lean beef
1 onion
1 tbsp. PU oil
3 tsps. paprika
1 small can tomatoes
1 tbsp. tomato purée
1 small green pepper
1 small sliced potato
¾ pint water
Salt
Ground black pepper

1 Cut beef into dice, chop onion and pepper.
2 Toss meat in hot oil to seal and fry until brown.
3 Add onion and peppers, and cook until they are soft.
4 Add paprika, tomatoes and liquor, potato, water, tomato purée, salt and pepper.
5 Cover and simmer until meat is tender, about 2 hr.
6 Adjust seasoning.

If possible leave 24 hr. in refrigerator before eating. Serve piping hot with hunks of crisp french bread. A favourite midday meal much enjoyed by skiing enthusiasts in the Austrian Alps.

Minestrone Soup

2 tbsps. PU oil
1 small onion
2 pieces celery
1 carrot
1 potato
2 cabbage leaves
1 leek
2 tomatoes
1 small turnip
1 bay leaf
1 level tsp. mixed dried herbs
2 oz. macaroni
Pinch of sugar
2 pints boiling water or chicken stock
Salt and pepper
1 oz. parmesan cheese

1 Peel and dice vegetables. Shred cabbage.
2 Sauté diced onions in oil.
3 Add all vegetables except cabbage and tomatoes and sauté 5 mins.
4 Add water or stock, bay leaf, herbs, salt, pepper and sugar.
5 Bring back to boil and add tomatoes and cabbage.
6 Cover and simmer 1 hr.
7 Add macaroni and continue cooking until tender.
8 Remove bay leaf and pour hot soup into tureen and sprinkle with parmesan cheese.

Cream of Mushroom Soup

2 tbsps. oil
2 tbsps. flour
1 pint skimmed milk
4 oz. mushrooms
1 chicken stock cube
Garlic powder
Salt and pepper
Mushroom ketchup

1 Blend oil, flour and ½ tsp. salt with a little of the milk. Add remainder of milk and slowly bring to boil stirring constantly.
2 Wash and chop mushrooms discarding stalks if tough.
3 Add mushrooms, stock cube and garlic to sauce.
4 Simmer 30 min. stirring frequently. Press through sieve or liquidize in electric blender.
5 Return to saucepan and season to taste with salt, pepper and a dash of mushroom ketchup.

Garlic is now obtainable in powder form which will keep indefinitely in a dry store cupboard. The chicken stock cube contains a small amount of fat but is quite permissible unless you are on a very strict non-fat diet.

Orange and Tomato Soup

2 lb. fresh or 2 cans tomatoes
1 medium carrot
1 medium onion
1 bay leaf
6 peppercorns
1 strip lemon rind
2½ pints chicken stock
1½ oz. PU margarine
1½ oz. flour
1 lump sugar
1 5-oz. carton non-fat yoghurt
¼ tsp. cornflour
1 tbsp. cold water
Pinch salt
1 orange
Salt and pepper

1 Slice onion and carrot finely and place in saucepan with tomatoes, bay leaf, lemon rind, peppercorns and stock. Add seasoning.
2 Bring to boil and simmer gently 1 hr.
3 Press through a sieve to remove pips, skin, etc.
4 Melt margarine in a pan. Add flour and cook 1 min.
5 Add tomato mixture and stir well.
6 Rub sugar lump over orange to remove and absorb zest, and place this sugar in soup.
7 Simmer 5 min. If not thick enough, for a little longer.
8 Pare rind from orange and cut into thin strips.
9 Blend cornflour with water and orange juice, and place in small pan with yoghurt.
10 Slowly bring to boil, stirring constantly and simmer 5 min. until thick.
11 Add yoghurt to soup and stir well. Keep hot.
12 Place thin strips of orange rind in boiling water and simmer 6 min. Drain and sprinkle over soup.

The yoghurt is thickened and cooked to prevent curdling when combined with the soup.

A recipe for chicken stock will be found at the end of the soup section.

If you have difficulty in removing the orange zest, first score the skin with a fork.

Tomato Soup

2 14-oz. cans of tomatoes (or 2 lb. fresh ripe tomatoes)
1 small (3-oz.) can tomato purée
1 large onion (finely chopped)
1 large potato, peeled and quartered
3 shakes worcestershire sauce
2 tsps. lemon juice
1 tsp. dried basil
1 bay leaf
Salt and pepper
1 pint water

1 Place all ingredients in large saucepan and bring to boil.
2 Cover with lid and simmer 1 hr.
3 Remove bay leaf and pass soup through a 'mouli' or sieve.
4 Adjust seasoning and serve.

If you have a pressure cooker, this soup can be ready in 20 min. It is an ideal slimmers' soup as there is no fat at all. By all means cook a double quantity and freeze for use later. This soup will keep in a refrigerator for several days but should be brought to the boil before serving.

Vichyssoise

1 lb. large leeks
1 oz. PU margarine
1½ pints fresh chicken stock
¾ lb. potatoes
1 stick celery
1 carton fat-free yoghurt
2 tsps. cornflour
A little water
Chopped chives
Salt and pepper

1 Discard all green parts of leeks and slice remaining white parts thinly.
2 Slice celery thinly.
3 Sauté leeks and celery gently in the margarine. DO NOT BROWN.
4 Peel and thinly slice potatoes and add to leeks with chicken stock.

5 Bring to boil, then simmer until tender, 15 min.
6 Press through a sieve or liquidize in electric blender. Season.
7 Blend cornflour with water and place in pan with yoghurt.
8 Bring slowly to boil, stirring carefully.
9 Combine yoghurt with soup.
10 Chill. Serve garnished with chopped chives.

Fresh stock must be used as the basis for this iced soup. Cheat if you like and serve hot. It is still very tasty that way.

Watercress Soup
2 bunches watercress
2 oz. flour
3 oz. PU margarine
2 tbsps. PU oil
1 large onion
½ pint skimmed milk
1 pint chicken stock
Salt and pepper

1 Wash watercress and remove 2 in. of stem.
2 Peel and chop onion.
3 Sauté onion in PU oil until soft, add watercress. Cover and cook 3 or 4 min.
4 Melt margarine in saucepan, stir in flour, add milk and stock gradually and bring slowly to boil stirring continuously. Add salt and pepper to taste.
5 Add watercress mixture to sauce and stir well.
6 Press through a sieve or liquidize.
7 Reheat and serve hot

Reconsituted dried onions can be used very adequately. Follow directions on packet, but generally pour boiling water over onions to cover. Leave for 10 min. and then strain when onions will be ready to sauté. About 1 tbsp. onions would be required in this recipe.

Beef Stock
1 lb. freshly bought marrow bone
1 bay leaf
Salt and pepper
2 pints water

1 Ask the butcher to chop up the bones.
2 Wash the bones in cold water.
3 Place all ingredients in large saucepan.
4 Cover and simmer 2 hr. until liquid is reduced by a quarter.
5 Strain, cool and refrigerate.
6 Remove any fat on surface when cold.

Unless you are freezing the stock, use within 24 hr. Bring to the boil and simmer 5 min. before using.

Chicken Stock
1 roast chicken carcase or chicken bones and flesh cooked or uncooked
1 bay leaf
Salt and pepper
2 pints water

1 Place all ingredients in large saucepan.
2 Bring to boil. Lower heat and simmer covered until liquid is reduced by a quarter.
3 Strain, cool and refrigerate until fat has solidified on surface.
4 Remove fat.
5 Use as required.
Always bring stock to boil and simmer 5 min. before using.

Fish Stock
Fresh fish bones and skin
1 pint water
1 tsp. salt
8 peppercorns
1 small onion, quartered
1 stick of celery
2 bay leaves
Pinch of mixed herbs

1 Place bones and skin in saucepan, add water and all other ingredients and slowly bring to boil.
2 Reduce heat and simmer 15 to 20 min.
3 Strain and use immediately.

Overcooked fish stock will turn bitter.

Vegetable Stock
2 lb. of mixture of any of the following vegetables:
carrot, celery, celeriac, spinach, turnip, cauliflower, onion, tomatoes
2 level tsps. salt
2 bay leaves
2 pints water

1 Scrub vegetables and dice. Do not peel.
2 Place in large saucepan with salt and bay leaves and cover with water.
3 Bring to boil and simmer 2 hr. Skim as necessary.
4 Pass through a sieve and press *gently* with wooden spoon.
5 Discard pulp.
6 Use stock as desired.

Light Court Bouillon
2 pints water
1 bay leaf
Few parsley stalks
1 onion, sliced
Juice of half a lemon
3 peppercorns
¼ pint skimmed milk
½ level tsp. salt

1 Place all ingredients in saucepan.
2 Bring to boil. Simmer 10 min.
3 Strain.
4 Leave to cool.
5 Use to poach any white fish.

4. Hors d'oeuvres and salads

American Grapefruit
1 large grapefruit
½ red apple
2 maraschino cherries

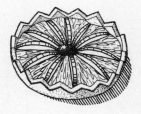

1 Halve grapefruit and loosen segments with a grapefruit knife.
2 Cut round outside of fruit to sever membranes.
3 Loosen core from underneath.
4 Remove membrane and core.
5 Vandyke edges.

Vandyke edges

6 Remove core from apple.

7 Thinly slice apple leaving skin on, and place a half slice between each segment of grapefruit.

8 Top with a cherry.

Florida Cocktail
2 grapefruit
2 jaffa oranges
Crushed ice (if available)
Freshly chopped mint

1 Using a very sharp knife and chopping board, remove slice from top and bottom of fruit to reveal flesh.

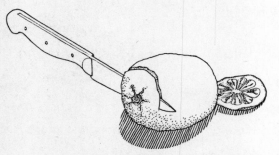

Peeling and segmenting fruit—1

2 Stand fruit cut side on board and remove remaining peel and pith following curve of fruit with knife.

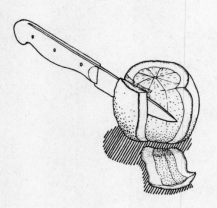

2

3 Taking great care hold fruit in palm of one hand and cut from outside to centre of each segment to remove flesh while leaving membrane.

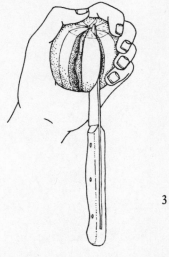

3

4 Place some crushed ice in glasses and arrange orange and grapefruit segments on top.
5 Serve chilled, sprinkled with chopped mint.

Sugar is only required if the oranges are sour. Ice cubes can be crushed in the liquidizer.

Melon Basket

1 green melon
Small amount colourful fruit, oranges, cherries, etc.
1 level tbsp. caster sugar
2 tsp. Grand Marnier (optional)

1 Remove small slice from base of melon so that the fruit will stand steadily.
2 Remove top of melon, cutting straight across about 2 in down from the point. De-seed melon.
3 Using teaspoon or melon baller, cut out balls, but do not cut too close to the walls of the melon.
4 Mix melon balls with other fruit, add sugar and liqueur.
5 Vandyke edge of melon base.

6 Fill base with fruit using decoratively.
7 Cut centre strip from top of melon and shave away surplus flesh.

Melon basket

8 Vandyke ends of strip and place this piece on top of the filled melon to form a handle.
9 Rub outside of melon with a little oil and serve on a platter surrounded by any surplus fruit.

The oil gives the outside of the melon a glorious shine.
Chill before serving as an hors d'oeuvre or dessert. Avoid soft mushy fruits such as raspberries, as the colour will run into the other fruits.

Artichokes *au Naturel*
1 globe artichoke per person
1 oz. PU margarine
Salt and pepper
Lemon juice

1 Cut stem off level with leaves.
2 Trim ½ in. from top of leaves.
3 Pull leaves open with thumbs to allow cold running water to wash thoroughly.
4 Place in boiling salted water to which a little lemon juice has been added. Cover with loosely fitting lid. Simmer 30 to 35 min.
5 Drain thoroughly and serve with melted seasoned PU margarine.

Artichokes are cooked when a leaf pulls away easily. A stainless steel knife or scissors should be used for cutting away tips.

Artichokes are low in calories. To eat, pull the leaves off one at a time, dip into sauce, then pull flesh away with your teeth. Discard leaves. Remove spiky part or choke, and eat the delicately flavoured bottom with a knife and fork.

Always provide a small dish of water with a lemon slice floating in it for guests to rinse their fingers.

Artichoke Vinaigrette

1 artichoke per person.
1 tbsp. french dressing (see page 119).

1 Cook as for Artichokes *au Naturel* (see previous recipe).
2 Drain and leave until cold.
3 Serve with french dressing.

Aubergine Salad

2 large or 4 small aubergines
1 red pepper
3 tbsps. wine vinegar
3 tbsps. PU oil
Salt and pepper
Garlic

1 Skin aubergines & cut into ½ in. cubes.
2 Cook in boiling salted water 7 min. Drain well.
3 Remove stalk and seeds from red pepper. Blanch in boiling water, simmer 3 min. Drain.
4 Chop into ½ in. squares and mix with aubergines.
5 Mix vinegar and oil with salt, pepper and garlic to taste.
6 Pour over vegetable mixture.
7 Leave 24 hr. before serving.

Avocado Salad

½ ripe avocado
2 carrots
1 raw beetroot
½ cucumber
2 tomatoes
4 spring onions
3 tbsps. french dressing (see page 119)

1 Peel carrots.
2 Peel cucumber.
3 Remove root end and most of stem from spring onions.
4 Peel beetroot.
5 Peel avocado.
6 Dice all ingredients into ¼ in. cubes.
7 Place in wooden bowl and pour dressing over.
8 Allow to stand in refrigerator 1 hr.
9 Mix again before serving.

Avocado is high in fat content each half pear having 100 calories. In this recipe 'addicts' will enjoy the flavour without that guilty feeling.

Caponatina Siciliana
4 medium aubergines
7½ fl. oz. PU oil
4 sliced onions
3 oz. can tomato purée
4 stalks celery, diced
2 tbsps. capers
4 pitted chopped olives
1 tbsp. pine nuts
2½ fl. oz. wine vinegar
2 tbsps. sugar
¾ tsp. salt
½ tsp. pepper

1 Peel and dice aubergines and sauté in the oil.
2 Remove aubergines from pan and drain.
3 Add sliced onions to oil in pan and gently brown.
4 Add tomato purée and celery and cook until celery is tender. Add a little water if necessary.
5 Add capers, olives, pine nuts and aubergines.
6 Heat vinegar in small saucepan, add sugar to dissolve.
7 Pour over aubergine mixture, add salt and pepper and simmer 20 min.

This eggplant hors d'oeuvre should be prepared 24 hr before eating and is served cold. It will keep (covered) in a refrigerator for 10 days.
When draining fried foods, use the matt side of brown

paper, brown paper bags or fish draining paper which can be purchased from good stationers under that name. Absorbent general purpose kitchen paper may be used, but foods should not rest on it for any length of time as it tends to stick when damp from condensation.

Chicory Walnut Salad
4 heads of chicory
2 eating apples
2 oz. fresh shelled walnuts
2 tbsps. PU oil
1 tbsp. wine vinegar
½ carton fat-free yoghurt
Pinch sugar
Salt and pepper

1 Remove outer leaves from chicory and slice thickly.
2 Chop walnuts.
3 Peel and chop apples.
4 Beat oil, vinegar and yoghurt together and season to taste.
5 Add chicory, walnuts and apples to dressing.
6 Serve chilled.

Cucumber Salad
1 Cucumber
French dressing (see page 119)
Chopped parsley

1 Peel cucumber and slice thinly.
2 Arrange slices overlapping in serving dish.
3 Spoon french dressing over cucumber slices.
4 Garnish with chopped parsley

Mushroom Salad
4 oz. mushrooms
3 tbsps. PU oil
1 tbsp. fresh lemon juice
4 finely chopped spring onions
Salt and pepper

1 Wash and slice mushrooms, discarding stalks.

2 Combine oil and lemon juice and mix with mushrooms, onions, salt and pepper.

Mushrooms contain only 5 calories to the ounce and are a palatable addition to any salad. Serve raw or cooked.

Salade Niçoise
1 10-oz. packet frozen whole green beans
1 cucumber
6 tomatoes
1 medium can tuna fish
1 can anchovy fillets
3 tbsps. skimmed milk
2 tsps. chopped chives
4 olives
2 tbsps. PU french dressing (see page 119)

1 Cook the beans in boiling salted water, following instructions on packet. Drain. Rinse in cold water.
2 Slice tomatoes and cucumber. Leave skin on.
3 Open and drain anchovies and tuna fish.
4 Soak anchovies in skimmed milk for 30 min. to remove salt. Drain.
5 Flake tuna fish.
6 Arrange tuna fish, tomatoes, cucumber and beans in layers in serving dish. Sprinkle each layer with chopped chives.
7 Pour french dressing over the dish.
8 Form a lattice on top of salad with anchovies.
9 Halve stoned olives and place in lattice spaces cut side down.

The fish in this salad must count as part of the daily intake of fish, meat or poultry.

Olives are not recommended being high in fat and calories, but one or two will not be harmful.

Salade Niçoise St. Tropez
¼ lettuce
2 tomatoes
¼ cucumber
1½ cooked beetroots
Green pepper

2 eggs
1 carrot
1 can anchovy fillets
3 tbsps. french dressing (see page 119)
3 tbsps. skimmed milk

1 Hard boil eggs, cool and discard yolks.
2 Chop egg whites.
3 Peel and de-seed tomatoes. Cut into strips.
4 De-seed pepper and cut into thin rings.
5 Dice cucumber and beetroot.
6 Grate carrot.
7 Wash and dry lettuce.
8 Open can anchovies, drain and soak strips in skimmed milk for 30 min. to remove salt.
9 Line bowl with lettuce leaves and add tomatoes, cucumber and beetroot.
10 Cover with grated carrot and place pepper rings on top.
11 Drain anchovies and form a lattice with the fillets.
12 Fill spaces with chopped egg white.
13 Pour over french dressing.
14 Serve with brown bread, PU margarine and lemon quarters.

Salmon Paté
1 8-oz. can red salmon
4 oz. PU margarine
2 oz. cottage cheese
1 tbsp. lemon juice
Black pepper
Salt
Watercress for garnish

1 Sieve cottage cheese into mixing bowl.
2 Remove skin and bones from fish and pound with a wooden spoon.
3 Beat all ingredients together, divide into individual soufflé dishes.
4 Garnish with watercress.

Serve chilled with melba toast.

Hot Smoked Salmon Savouries

4 oz. plain flour
2 oz. PU margarine
Cold skimmed milk to mix

1 tbsp. PU oil
2 level tbsps. plain flour
½ pint skimmed milk

1 level tsp. paprika
1 level tsp. lemon juice
½ level tsp. white pepper
2 oz. smoked salmon

Parsley for garnish

1 Keeping all ingredients as cool as possible, rub PU margarine into flour.
2 Add sufficient cold milk to mix to a manageable dough.
3 Place dough in a polythene bag and leave to rest in refrigerator 30 min.
4 Roll paste thinly, cut into circles and place in patty or bun tins.
5 Return to freezer or coldest part of refrigerator until quite hard.
6 Prepare sauce. Blend PU oil and flour in small saucepan over low heat. Gradually add milk and bring to boil stirring continuously.
7 When sauce is thick, stir in lemon juice, paprika and white pepper and smoked salmon, finely chopped.
8 Leave chilled pastry cases in tins and fill with salmon mixture. The filling will not spread very much.
9 Bake in a preheated oven, 400 or 6, 15 to 20 min.
10 Garnish with a sprig of parsley.

Yield is about sixteen. Uncooked pastry freezes very well. When required, fill with freshly prepared filling, cook and serve hot.

Anchovies may be substituted or, if obtainable, gaffel-bitter, a Norwegian smoked herring which has a slightly sweet flavour and is sold canned.

If a softer filling is preferred, bake the pastry cases 'blind' and spoon in hot salmon mixture just before serving.

Hot Spaghetti Cocktail

8 oz. spaghetti
1 small can tuna fish
1 small can tomatoes
1 tbsp. chopped basil (preferably fresh)
3 tbsps. PU oil
Salt and pepper
Lemon butterflies (see page 184)

1 Liquidize tomatoes or press through a sieve.
2 Drain tuna fish, remove skin, and chop roughly.
3 Mix sieved tomato, tuna fish, basil, oil salt and pepper.
4 Cook spaghetti in boiling salted water until just tender. Drain well.
5 Mix spaghetti with sauce and divide between warmed individual dishes.
6 Garnish with lemon butterflies.

Taramasalata

6 oz. smoked cod's roe
2 oz. slice of stale white bread (crusts removed)
1 tbsp. grated onion
Garlic (optional)
1 tbsp. lemon juice
6 tbsps. PU oil
Skimmed milk

1 Soak bread in milk and squeeze until dry.
2 Pound into a paste with the cod's roe.
3 Add onion and garlic.
4 Beat in the oil and lemon juice gradually until mixture lightens.
5 Serve with melba toast.

An electric beater will produce the best results. The mixture should be fluffy and a very light pink. The above quantity of cod's roe, which may be purchased fresh or in a jar, is equivalent to one egg yolk. This quantity, however, will serve six to eight as a starter.

Garnish with slices of fresh tomato, lettuce and cucumber.

Tomato Salad

4 firm tomatoes
2 tbsps. french dressing (see page 119)
2 tsps. red wine (beaujolais)
1 tsp. basil

1 Wash tomatoes and slice thinly.
2 Arrange slices overlapping in serving dish.
3 Add wine to french dressing.
4 Spoon dressing over tomatoes.
5 Sprinkle with basil.

Waldorf Salad

2 red dessert apples
¾ oz. chopped walnuts
1 stick celery heart
2 tbsps. mayonnaise (see below)
Cress

1 Wash apples but do not peel.
2 Quarter and core.
3 Slice apples thinly.
4 Chop celery.
5 Mix nuts, celery and apple with mayonnaise.
6 Place in serving dish and garnish with cress.

Mayonnaise contains egg yolk, but if made with PU oil, there is only 16 mg. cholesterol in this recipe. Some slimmers, commercial mayonnaises do not contain egg yolk but oil content is not always given.

Winter Salad

1 small white cabbage
1 onion
1 large carrot
1 red apple
1 carton non-fat yoghurt
2 tbsps. PU oil
2 tbsps. lemon juice
Salt and pepper

1 Wash and shred cabbage.

2 Peel and chop onion.
3 Scrape and grate carrot.
4 Remove apple core, chop apple unpeeled.
5 Combine cabbage, onion, carrot and apple
6 Blend remaining ingredients and stir in to mixture.

5. Vegetables and vegetarian dishes

Asparagus

1 bundle Asparagus

1 Remove 2 in of woody end from stalks.
2 Scrape stalks lightly.
3 Tie in bundle with string.
4 Choose a saucepan to fit bundle of asparagus when standing upright.
5 Half fill with boiling salted water. Place asparagus in saucepan, tips uppermost and cover with lid.
6 Simmer 15 to 20 min. until tips are tender.
7 Drain gently to avoid breaking off tips.

Serve hot with melted seasoned PU margarine or cold with french dressing.

Aubergine Baskets

1 large aubergine
4 tomatoes
1 tbsp. chopped onion
2 heaped tbsps. chunky beef flavoured soya protein
½ pint vegetable stock
Bay leaf
Salt and pepper

1 Cut aubergine in half lengthways.
2 Sprinkle flesh with salt and score with a sharp knife. Leave aside 30 min. to 'de-gorge'.

3 Skin tomatoes and quarter.
4 Pour stock into saucepan and bring to boil.
5 Lower heat and add tomatoes, onion, soya protein, bay leaf, salt and pepper.
6 Cover and simmer 20 min.
7 Rinse aubergine under cold running water.
8 Scoop out flesh with grapefruit knife. Do not cut through skins.
9 Roughly chop aubergine flesh and add to mixture in pan.
10 Simmer 15 min. Remove bay leaf.
11 Pile hot mixture into aubergine skins in ovenproof dish.
12 Cover with greased greaseproof paper and bake 375 or 5; 20 min.

Serve with chipped potatoes (fried in PU oil).

Aubergine baskets provide a completely non-fat non-cholesterol high protein dish, and are suitable at any meal but particularly after too much 'dining-out' and you wish to repair the 'damage'.

Aubergine Fritters
1 large aubergine
4 tsps. soya flour
3 tbsps. plain flour
Scant ¼ pint skimmed milk
Pinch nutmeg
Salt and pepper
3 heaped tbsps. fresh brown breadcrumbs
PU oil for deep fat frying

1 Wash the aubergines and cut into ¼ in. thick slices. Do not peel.
2 Make batter from soya flour, flour, skimmed milk, nutmeg, salt and pepper.
3 Dip aubergine slices in batter and then coat with breadcrumbs.
4 Pat crumbs into slices with palette knife.
5 Deep fat fry at 360 to 375°F until golden brown.
6 Drain on absorbent kitchen paper and serve hot as a light supper dish or vegetable.

Aubergine Soufflé

1 large or 2 small aubergines
Salt
1 oz. PU margarine
1 tbsp. PU oil
1 tsp. soya flour
1 oz. plain flour
Scant ¼ pint (5 fl. oz.) skimmed milk .
Salt and pepper
5 egg whites

1 Preheat oven 375 or 5.
2 Cut aubergines in half longways. Make criss cross slits on open flesh with sharp knife and sprinkle liberally with salt. Leave 30 min.
3 Prepare panada. Blend flour, soya flour, oil and milk in saucepan. Bring to boil over low heat, stirring constantly. Cook until sauce is very thick and leaves the sides of the pan. Season.
4 Cover with wet disc of greaseproof paper placed on surface of sauce.
5 Rinse aubergine under cold water. Remove skin, and chop flesh into small pieces.
6 Sauté aubergine in PU margarine until soft. After 5 min. cover pan tightly with lid and lower heat. Leave to cook 20 min.
7 Liquidize aubergine, or mash thoroughly.
8 Combine aubergine mixture with sauce, adjust seasoning.
9 Beat egg whites until stiff but not dry.
10 Stir 1 tbsp. egg whites into purée. Fold in remainder of egg white.
11 Turn into greased 7 in. soufflé dish. Bake centre of oven oven 30 min. until set on top.

Do not open oven during first 15 min. and preferably not at all.

Aubergine soufflé may be baked in individual dishes at the same temperature but less cooking time will be needed.

Continental Cabbage

1 fresh cabbage
2 onions
½ clove of garlic, crushed

1 tbsp. PU oil
2 tomatoes, skinned
½ pint vegetable stock
1 level tbsp. flour
Salt and pepper

1 Cut cabbage into quarters and wash under cold running water.
2 Half fill large saucepan with water, bring to boil and blanche cabbage 3 min. Drain.
3 Slice onions and sauté in PU oil with garlic until soft but not coloured.
4 Slice tomatoes and add to pan.
5 Stir in flour and when blended, add stock. Bring to boil to thicken, stirring constantly. Season to taste.
6 Arrange cabbage on base of casserole and pour thickened stock over.
7 Cover and cook in oven 350 or 4. Approx. 1 hr.
Choose a cabbage whose leaves are tight.

Glazed Carrots
1 lb. carrots
2 oz. PU margarine
2 tbsps. water
1 tsp. chopped parsley
Salt and pepper
Pinch sugar

1 Scrape carrots and slice thinly.
2 Place in saucepan with PU margarine, water, parsley, salt and pepper.
3 Cover with well-fitting lid and cook over gentle heat. 15 min. Shake the pan occasionally.
4 Remove lid, add sugar and cook rapidly until water has evaporated.

Cauliflower Polonaise
1 medium-sized cauliflower
3 oz. PU margarine
3 heaped tbsps. breadcrumbs
1 tbsp. chopped parsley

1 Wash cauliflower in cold salted water.
2 Discard outer leaves. Cook cauliflower in boiling salted water until just tender. Drain.
3 Divide into sprigs and reassemble in serving dish. Keep hot.
4 Fry breadcrumbs in PU margarine until golden brown.
5 Spread over cauliflower and sprinkle with chopped parsley.

Corn on the Cob
1 corn cob per person
½ oz. PU margarine
Salt and pepper

1 Remove husk and silk from corn.
2 Place corn in pan of unsalted boiling water. Cook 15 to 20 min.
3 Drain. Dab with PU margarine and season at table.

Do not cook in salted water as this toughens the kernels. Fresh corn has firm white kernels which will pop if pierced with your fingernail.

Buttered Courgettes
½ lb. courgettes
1 oz. PU margarine
Nutmeg
Salt and pepper

1 Wash and dry courgettes. Cut away and discard top and bottom.
2 Leave unskinned and cut into 1 in. chunks.
3 Place in saucepan with salt and pepper and nutmeg and PU margarine.
4 Cover pan with sheet of foil and place lid on top.
5 Stand saucepan over very *low* heat and allow to cook gently.
6 Occasionally shake saucepan to prevent burning.
7 Cook until soft but not mushy. Approx. 30 min.

Choose firm courgettes. Soft courgettes tend to be bitter. Perhaps the title is a little unfair but taking into account the purpose of this book readers should be happy to accept the substitute. Of course use butter for non-heart-watchers.

Dhal

8 oz. lentils
2 pints boiling water
1 tbsp. PU oil
1 small onion, chopped
¼ tsp. chilli powder
½ tsp. turmeric powder
¼ tsp. garam masala
1 tsp. salt

1 Wash the lentils thoroughly in several changes of cold water.
2 Drain and put in a saucepan covered with the boiling water. Leave to soak 2 or 3 hours.
3 Add turmeric, chilli powder and salt, and cook lentils in the same water until tender. Boil a little faster towards the end of the cooking time if the mixture seems too lipuid. It should resemble a thin porridge.
4 Fry the onion and garam masala in the PU oil until the onions are brown.
5 Stir into the dhal and cook for 5 min.

Serve hot as an accompaniment to curry.

Lentils are a protein food and may be cooked without the curry seasonings until thick and made into croquettes.

Alternatively this recipe can be thinned down with stock and flavoured with a bouquet garni to make a winter soup.

Guru Pie

2 lb. mixed vegetables chosen from the following:
swedes, turnips, onions, carrots, leeks, celeriac, potatoes, parsnips
4 oz. mushrooms
2 oz. PU margarine
1 14 oz. can tomatoes
½ pint skimmed milk

1 oz. cornflour
1 tsp. yeast extract
1 level tsp. mixed dried herbs
Salt and pepper
1 oz. parmesan cheese
8 oz. wholemeal pastry

1 Peel and dice vegetables.
2 Sweat vegetables (except tomatoes) in PU fat. 10 min.
3 Add tomatoes, mushrooms and liquor, cover with lid and cook a further 10 min. Season to taste.
4 Stir in yeast extract and herbs.
5 Blend cornflour with a little of the cold milk. Add remainder of milk and pour onto vegetables.
6 Bring to boil to thicken, stirring all the time.
7 Turn into pie dish and sprinkle with cheese.
8 Damp edges of pie dish with water and cover with pastry.
9 Brush pastry with PU milk. Bake 400 or 6; 45 min.

Wholemeal Pastry
8 oz. wholemeal flour
Pinch salt
4 oz. PU margarine
Approx. 3 tbsps. skimmed milk

1 Sieve flour and salt into mixing bowl.
2 Rub in PU margarine until mixture resembles breadcrumbs.
3 Add sufficient cold skimmed milk to mix.
4 Chill 30 min. before rolling.
5 Use for fruit, vegetable or meat pies and bake for 35 to 40 mins, 425 or 7.

Best results in pastry making are obtained if PU margarine is stored in a freezer.

Braised Leeks

12 firm fresh leeks (1 in. to 1½ in. diameter)
¾ pint chicken or vegetable stock
2 oz. PU margarine
Salt and pepper

1 Cut off root of leek and strip away withered leaves.
2 Trim away top part to leave each leek 6 to 7 in. long.
3 Cut only green part in half lengthways stopping as it shades into white.
4 Wash thoroughly under cold running water.
5 Arrange leeks in one or two layers in heavy saucepan.
6 Pour in stock, add PU margarine. Bring to boil. Simmer 15 min., basting occasionally until white part is tender.
7 Preheat oven, 325 or 3.
8 Place leeks in one layer in greased roasting dish.
9 Taste stock and correct seasoning.
10 Pour over leeks, cover lightly with aluminium foil.
11 Bake 20 min. Leeks should be lightly coloured and stock almost evaporated. If there is very much stock remaining, remove leeks to serving dish. Pour stock into saucepan and boil rapidly to reduce.
12 Spoon a little reduced stock over leeks.

Creamed Leeks

4 large leeks
1 oz. plain flour
1 tbsp. PU oil
½ pint stock
Salt and pepper

1 Trim leeks, split lengthways and soak in cold salted water 15 min.
2 Drain and wash under cold running water.
3 Place in pan and cover with boiling stock.
4 Simmer until tender, 10 to 15 min.
5 Drain, retaining stock. Place leeks on hot serving dish.
6 Blend PU oil with flour in saucepan, whisk in ½ pint stock gradually. Place over low heat and whisk until sauce boils and thickens.
7 Add seasoning.
8 Coat leeks with sauce and serve as hot hors d'oeuvre supper dish, or vegetable accompaniment.

Braised Lettuce

6 round lettuce hearts
4 oz. PU margarine
20 spring onions or small pickling onions
Bouquet garni
Pepper and salt
½ tsp. sugar

1 Melt half of the margarine in a deep pan, add onions with a pinch of salt and ½ tsp. sugar.
2 Stir gently, until onions are coated and turn a golden colour. Remove onions and drain.
3 Cut lettuces in half lengthways, wash and dry.
4 Arrange lettuce halves in an oven proof casserole with remainder of margarine. Put in oven to melt margarine.
5 When margarine is melted, baste lettuce and sprinkle with salt and pepper.
6 Place onions in centre of lettuce with bouquet garni.
7 Cover casserole and braise in oven 30 min. 325 or 3
8 If too much liquor forms, remove lid for last 10 min. Remove bouquet garni before serving.

A charming summer vegetable to accompany grills.

Stuffed Marrow

1 large marrow
1 tbsp. PU oil
1 large onion
6 oz. lean minced beef
4 tomatoes
1 tbsp. chopped parsley
2 oz. fresh breadcrumbs
1 oz. parmesan cheese
Pinch dry mustard
Salt and pepper

1 Peel and chop onion, skin and chop tomatoes.
2 Fry onion and minced beef gently in PU oil until light brown.
3 Add tomatoes, parsley, breadcrumbs, cheese, mustard, salt and pepper. Remove from heat, taste, and adjust seasoning.

4 Cut 1 in. from one end of marrow. Set aside.
5 Scoop out seeds.
6 Half fill large saucepan with water, salt, and bring to boil.
7 Gently lower marrow and end into saucepan, lower heat and simmer 4 min. (depending on size of marrow).
8 Drain well. Pack cavity with beef mixture.
9 Replace marrow end and insert wooden cocktail sticks to secure.
10 Wrap in foil or roaster-bag, place in ovenproof dish. Bake 375 or 5, approx. 45 min.
11 Unwrap and turn on to hot serving dish.
12 Coat with espagnole sauce.

For a vegetarian or lower cholesterol meal substitute minced beef flavoured soya protein. Reconstitute with water before frying, to which 1 tsp. of yeast extract has been added.

Mushroom Flan

Pastry   4 oz. plain flour
3 oz. PU margarine
Cold water
Pinch of salt

Filling   2 egg whites
¼ pint buttermilk (fat free)
Small onion
4 oz. mushrooms
1 tbsp. PU oil
Salt and pepper
2 tsps. mushroom ketchup

1 Prepare pastry. Rub 1½ oz. margarine into flour and salt, until it resembles breadcrumbs. Add cold water and mix to a paste with palette knife. Knead lightly, cover and place in refrigerator for 30 min.
2 Light oven, 400 or 6
3 Roll paste into oblong shape three times as long as wide.
4 Place remaining 1½ oz. margarine in dabs over two thirds paste.

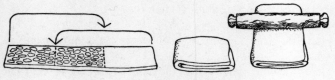

Mushroom flan

5 Fold bottom section up over middle and then top section down over middle to form a three layer dough.

6 Turn paste sideways (open end towards you) and roll into original length.

7 Repeat folding as in 5 and then roll pastry into round, 1 in. wider than flan ring.

8 Fit pastry into 6 in flan ring and bake blind for 10 min.

9 Chop onion and slice mushrooms and sauté in oil until soft but not brown.

10 Beat egg whites with buttermilk, add salt, pepper and mushroom ketchup.

11 Remove foil from pastry case and lower oven heat to 325 or 3

12 Pour filling into pastry case and bake on middle shelf, 45 min.

To test for cooking—pierce filling with a sharp knife and if mixture does not ooze liquid remove flan from oven. It will continue to cook as it cools.

This type of filling takes longer to cook than a conventional quiche because it is more difficult for egg whites to coagulate on their own.

Instructions for lining a flan ring and 'baking blind' will be found in the 'How to . . . ' chapter.

Mushroom Pielets

4 oz. mushrooms
1 tomato
2 tbsps. PU oil
1 large can butter beans
Juice of ½ lemon
2 tsps. tomato purée
Dash worcestershire sauce
1 oz. grated cheese

1 oz. fresh breadcrumbs
Salt and pepper
1 tsp. chopped parsley

1 Wash and chop mushrooms.
2 Skin and chop tomato.
3 Drain beans and discard liquor.
4 Sauté mushrooms and tomatoes in oil.
5 Crush beans and add to mixture with lemon juice, tomato purée, worcestershire sauce, salt and pepper.
6 Place in individual fireproof dishes or scallop shells.
7 Mix breadcrumbs, cheese and parsley and sprinkle on top.
8 Brown under hot grill until topping is crisp.

Serve as an hors d'oeuvre or light supper dish with a green salad accompaniment.

Nut Cutlets

2 oz. grated mixed nuts (not cashew or peanuts)
1 oz. fresh breadcrumbs
1 small onion (grated)
1 small potato (grated)
½ oz. PU margarine
½ oz. flour
⅛ pint skimmed milk
1 tsp. yeast extract

Coating
1 tbsp. skimmed milk
2 egg whites
1 oz. fresh breadcrumbs

1 Melt PU margarine in saucepan over gentle heat.
2 Stir in flour. Add milk and blend.
3 Bring to boil stirring constantly until a thick sauce or panada is formed. Season to taste. Stir in yeast extract.
4 Remove from heat. Add nuts, breadcrumbs, potato and onion. Leave to cool.
5 With floured hands form into shapes to resemble a lamb chop.
6 Beat 1 tbsp. skimmed milk and egg whites together.
7 Dip cutlets in this and then coat with breadcrumbs.
8 Repeat this process pressing well in with palette knife.
9 Fry in deep or shallow fat until brown.

Onion Bhaggia

2 large onions
1 level tsp. curry powder
Salt
4 level tbsps. 'gram' flour
Cold water to mix
PU oil for frying

1 Peel and slice onions thinly.
2 Mix curry powder, approx. ½ tsp. salt, gram flour and sufficient cold water to form a very thick batter.
3 Stir in onions so that they are all well covered.
4 Half fill saucepan with PU oil and heat to 365°F.
5 Gently drop dessertspoons full of mixture into oil making sure onions are completely immersed.
6 Fry until brown. Drain and serve hot.

For those who dislike curry, use half the quantity of curry powder, but do not omit altogether.
Left-overs may be reheated in the oven.
Gram flour is obtainable from Indian or African grocers and is made from split-peas.
Curry powder and garam masala (a fuller-flavoured powder) are stocked by most grocers.

Peas and Onions

1 tbsp. PU oil
1 small chopped onion
½ lb. shelled fresh or frozen peas
½ pint stock (see under stocks, pages 33–34)
Salt and pepper
Pinch of sugar
Mint
Dab PU margarine

1 Sauté onion in PU oil in saucepan.
2 Add other ingredients.
3 Stir and simmer until cooked.
4 Add dab of PU margarine.
5 Serve hot.

Ten min. is all you need to allow if using frozen peas. Fresh peas will require 20 min. after adding to onion.

Pommes Anna

12 oz. peeled potatoes
1 oz. PU margarine
Salt and pepper
A few sprigs parsley

1 Grease a 7 in. sandwich tin.
2 Slice the potatoes in very thin circles.
3 Place a layer of prepared potatoes overlapping in the base of the tin.
4 Spread with some PU margarine and season.
5 Cover with another layer of potato and repeat until mixture nearly reaches top of tin.
6 Cover with an ovenproof plate. Bake in preheated oven, 375 or 5, approx. 30 min. Remove plate and continue to bake for 10 min.
7 Turn out onto hot serving dish. Garnish with parsley.

If your diet allows, the layers of potato may be sprinkled with a little grated cheese.

Duchesse Potato

¾ lb. peeled potatoes
1 egg white
¾ oz. PU margarine
Salt and pepper
Grated nutmeg

1 Boil potatoes until cooked. Drain. Return to saucepan.
2 Mash with potato masher or fork. Add PU margarine and seasoning. If mixture is too wet, stir over low heat for a few moments.
3 Leave to cool a little.
4 Add egg white. Beat well.
5 Place in forcing bag fitted with large star nozzle.
6 Pipe into rosettes on greased baking sheet.
7 Brown in oven 425 or 7, or under grill.

Jacket Potatoes—Duxelles

4 large unblemished potatoes
4 oz. mushrooms
1 small shallot

Pinch oregano
Pinch salt
Pinch pepper
1 oz. PU margarine
½ tsp. yeast extract
2 tsps. red wine

1 Scrub and prick potatoes. Bake in oven 400 or 6. Approx. 1 hr. (the potatoes should be placed near the top of the oven on an oven rack).
2 Wash and chop the mushrooms and shallot finely.
3 Sauté in PU margarine with the oregano, salt and pepper until liquid has evaporated.
4 Add yeast extract and wine. Continue cooking until the mixture forms a paste. Taste and adjust seasoning.
5 When potatoes are cooked, remove from oven and cut in half lengthways.
6 Mash potatoes in their skins and form a slight hollow.
7 Fill with mushroom paste.

Serve hot with a green salad.
Potatoes will burst if they are insufficiently pricked.

Potato Nests
1 lb. potatoes
1 egg white
Salt and pepper
Nutmeg
1 tbsp. PU oil

1 Scrub and peel potatoes. Cut into small even pieces.
2 Cook until tender in salted boiling water.
3 Drain thoroughly.
4 Sieve potatoes.
5 Beat in salt, pepper, nutmeg and oil.
6 Place mixture in a large forcing bag fitted with a large star tube.
7 Pipe potato into nest shapes on a lightly greased baking tray.

8 Brush with egg white.
9 Bake until golden brown and crisp, 425 or 7; 7 to 10 min.
10 Fill with cooked macedoine of vegetables.

The shape of a 'nest' is similar to a 3 in. vol-au-vent case.

Quick Pizza
1 large can tomatoes
1 tbsp. PU oil
1 clove of garlic, crushed
Salt and pepper
8 oz. self-raising flour
½ tsp. salt
1 level tsp. baking powder
2 oz. PU margarine
¼ pint skimmed milk
1 can anchovy fillets
6 pitted olives
1 oz. grated cheese

1 Empty can of tomatoes into a saucepan, add PU oil,
   garlic, salt and pepper. Simmer 30 min. until tomatoes
   pulp and mixture thickens.
2 Sieve flour, baking powder and salt into mixing bowl.
3 Rub in PU margarine.
4 Add milk to form a soft dough.
5 Knead dough gently on floured board. Form a ball.
6 Roll or press onto 9 in. greased pie plate.
7 Top with tomato mixture.
8 Arrange drained anchovy fillets and sliced olives in lattice
   design on surface.
9 Sprinkle with cheese
10 Bake 375 or 5; 45 min.

Chopped ham and gherkins may replace anchovies and
olives if preferred.

Ratatouille

2 green peppers
½ lb. courgettes
1 large aubergine
½ lb. tomatoes
1 large onion
1 clove of garlic, crushed
2 tbsps. red wine
4 tbsps. PU oil
Salt and pepper

1 Peel and slice onion, remove core and seeds from peppers and cut in ¼ in. thick rings.
2 Cut aubergine into thin slices, top and tail courgettes and divide into 1 in. chunks.
3 Skin and roughly chop tomatoes.
4 Fry onion and garlic in PU oil until soft.
5 Add peppers courgettes and aubergine and continue to fry gently, approx. 10 min.
6 Stir in tomatoes, wine and seasoning. Cover tightly and simmer over very low heat for at least 1 hr.

Add a little water if mixture becomes too dry.
The vegetables should be soft but not allowed to disintegrate.
Serve hot as a vegetable accompaniment to meat dishes or cold as an hors d'oeuvres.

Boiled Rice

2 oz. long-grain rice per person
Water

1 Place rice in sieve and run cold water through to remove starch.
2 When rice changes colour from white to transluscent, turn into a pan half filled with boiling salted water.
3 Stir once and boil uncovered until cooked. 10–12 min.
4 Turn immediately into sieve and again run under cold water to remove remainder of starch, and to separate the grains.
5 Shake well and turn into dish.
6 Place in oven 325 or 3; 10 min. or until warm and dry.
7 Fluff with fork.

Use a good long-grain rice such as American long grain, patna or basmatti. Round rice is only suitable for sweet dishes. Rice keeps for a few days in a refrigerator, but then turns sour. Never store cooked rice in aluminium foil for the foil becomes pitted and tiny metal pieces adhere to the rice.

Steaming in a sieve over boiling water is a good method of reheating.

To test if the the rice is cooked, press a grain between the thumb and forefinger and the grain should squash under hard pressure—or pop it into your mouth to test.

Spaghetti Napolitana

8 oz. spaghetti
1 tsp. PU oil

Tomato sauce
1 chopped onion
1 crushed clove of garlic
2 tbsps. PU oil
Bay leaf
Large can tomatoes

2 tsps. bottled pesto *or*
1 level tsp. ground pine nuts
1 level tsp. dried basil
1 level tsp. parmesan cheese
1 level tsp. PU oil

1 tbsp. parmesan cheese
Salt and pepper

1 Drain tomatoes and set liquor aside.
2 Fry onions and garlic in oil until golden brown.
3 Reduce heat and add tomatoes. Crush with wooden spoon or potato masher.
4 Add bay leaf, salt, pepper and 2 tbsps. tomato liquor.
5 Simmer, stirring occasionally, 30 min.
6 Stir in pesto or pesto ingredients.
7 Cook until sauce is thick.
8 Cook spaghetti in boiling salted water to which a tsp. of PU oil has been added.
9 When spaghetti is cooked (that is when a strand of spaghetti can just be cut with the side of a fork), drain and place in a hot dish.

10 Remove bay leaf from sauce. Pour sauce over spaghetti and sprinkle with cheese.

Use remaining tomato liquor in vegetable stock or soups.
Pesto is obtainable at specialist Italian grocers, is not expensive and keeps well. You can make up a quantity yourself by increasing the ingredients listed when these should be pounded together until they emulsify.

Christmas Sprouts
2 lb. sprouts
8 oz. skinned chestnuts, canned or freshly boiled
2 oz. PU margarine
Salt to taste

1 Discard base and outer leaves of sprouts.
2 Wash in cold salted water and cut a cross on base of stalk with sharp knife.
3 Cook sprouts in boiling salted water until just tender. Drain.
4 Toss chestnuts in melted PU margarine over moderate heat. Chop roughly and add sprouts to saucepan.
5 Reheat for 2 or 3 min., stirring gently.
6 Turn into hot serving dish.

Tomatoes gratinées
1 lb. firm tomatoes
2 tbsps. fresh breadcrumbs
1 tbsp. parmesan cheese
2 tsps. basil
1 small chopped onion
1 tbsp. PU oil
Salt and pepper

1 Cut tomatoes in half and place in greased ovenproof dish.
2 Brush tops with oil and sprinkle with salt and pepper.
3 Mix breadcrumbs, cheese, basil and finely chopped onion together, and spoon over tomatoes.
4 Bake 350 or 4; 20 to 30 min.

This makes an interesting hot hors d'oeuvre or serve as a vegetable, when the meat portions are small.

Vegetable Cutlets

2 oz. peas
2 oz. green beans
1 small onion, chopped
2 oz. peeled potatoes
2 oz. cauliflower
Salt
Pinch chilli powder
Pinch paprika
Pinch curry powder
Pinch ground ginger
1 level tbsp. chopped parsley
½ oz. PU margarine
½ oz. flour
⅛ pt. (2½ fl. oz.) skimmed milk
1 oz. flour for dredging
PU oil for frying

1 Place all vegetables in boiling salted water and cook until tender. Drain.
2 Press through a sieve, or mince. Add spices and parsley.
3 Melt PU margarine in small saucepan. Stir in flour and gradually blend in skimmed milk. Bring to boil, stirring all the time until a thick sauce is formed.
4 Mix sauce, mashed vegetables and parsley together.
5 Taste and adjust seasoning.
6 Shape into cutlets and dredge with flour. Leave to cool a little.
7 Fry in shallow oil until golden brown, turning once.
8 Serve hot, with tomato sauce or curry sauce.

A lightly spiced vegetarian cutlet which may be served as a supper dish or vegetable accompaniment to curried beef, chicken or lamb.
This quantity makes six cutlets.

Individual Yorkshire Puddings

4 oz. plain or strong flour
1 tbsp. PU oil
½ level tsp. salt
2 egg whites
½ pint skimmed milk

1 Preheat oven 450 or 8.
2 Thoroughly grease twelve bun or patty tins.
3 Place flour in mixing bowl and gradually add milk, oil and salt, to form a batter.
4 Lightly beat egg whites, add to batter and beat thoroughly.
5 Pour mixture into individual tins about three quarters full.
6 Bake at once, near top of oven. Approx. 15 min.

Do not open the oven for the first 10 min. of cooking time.

To avoid spilling batter pour into jug before filling small tins.

Mixed vegetables in hot yoghurt sauce

1 lb. mixed frozen vegetables
1 small onion
1 carton low fat yoghurt
½ oz. PU margarine
Salt and pepper

1 Place mixed vegetables in saucepan of boiling salted water. Bring back to boil and cook until tender. 7 to 10 min.
2 Finely chop onion. Place in small saucepan with PU margarine. Cook gently over low heat, 5 min.
3 Stir in carton of yoghurt, salt and pepper. Heat slowly.
4 Drain vegetables and toss in yoghurt sauce.
5 Serve hot.

Sweet corn may be substituted for mixed vegetables.

6. Fish

Poached Cod
4 cod steaks (1½ lb.)
2 pints light court bouillon (see page 34)
Lemon butterflies (see page 184)
Sprigs of parsley

1 Wash the fish.
2 Pour court bouillon into large saucepan. Bring to boil.
3 Gently lower cod steaks into liquid. Simmer 10 to 12 min.
4 Drain. Serve garnished with parsley and lemon butter-flies.

Serve with boiled or creamed potatoes and sliced carrots.
Allow 8 min. per pound for poaching fish.

Cider Halibut
1 lb. halibut fillet
¼ pint cider
1 large onion (peeled and chopped)
1½ oz. PU margarine
1 oz. flour
½ pint skimmed milk
Salt and pepper
2 tsps. fresh chopped parsley

1 Skin fish.
2 Place fish and skin in frying pan and cover with cider.
3 Gently poach until cooked, approx. 8 min.

4 Melt margarine in pan and sauté onion until soft, 10 min.
5 Stir in flour, then gradually add milk.
6 Bring to boil. Season and cover. Simmer 5 min.
7 Add parsley to sauce.
8 Remove fish from liquor and place in ovenproof dish.
9 Discard skin. Boil liquor until reduced by half.
10 Stir fish liquor into sauce.
11 Pour sauce over fish and brown under grill.

Fish Cakes
1 lb. white fish fillet
¾ lb. potatoes
2 tbsps. minced onion
2 tbsps. PU oil
Salt and pepper
Lemon juice
Flour for dredging

1 Poach fillets in water and lemon juice until flaky.
2 Remove skin and bones and flake fish.
3 Scrub and peel potatoes, boil and mash.
4 Combine fish, potatoes, onion, salt, pepper and oil, and form into flattish cakes. Dredge with flour.
5 Shallow fry in PU oil, 6 min., turning once.
6 Drain well.

As a variation try

Anchovy Fish Cakes
1 can anchovy fillets
Skimmed milk
Other ingredients as listed above

1 Drain anchovies and soak in milk for 30 min.
2 Dry the anchovies, cut into thin strips and mix with fish cake ingredients before shaping.

When preparing Anchovy Fish Cakes, less salt will be required in basic mixture.

Fish Pie

1 lb. white fish fillet
½ pint parsley sauce (see page 118)
1 lb. cooked mashed potato
1 oz. PU margarine
Salt and pepper
Lemon juice

1 Poach fish in seasoned water with lemon juice until white and flaky. 8 min.
2 Flake fish. Remove skin and bones.
3 Blend fish with parsley sauce and place in greased pie dish.
4 Blend mashed potato with PU margarine. Add seasoning.
5 Spread or pipe over fish mixture.
6 Bake 400 or 6; 25 to 30 min.

Anchovy sauce may be used instead of parsley sauce.

Haddock Cutlets Esquadore

4 cutlets of fresh haddock
1 onion
1 lb. tomatoes
¼ pint dry white wine
1 level tbsp. plain flour
1 level tsp. dried basil
1 level tsp. castor sugar
1 level tbsp. chopped capers
1 oz. PU margarine
1 tbsp. PU oil
Salt and pepper
Garlic powder

1 Peel and slice onion, skin and slice tomatoes.
2 Sauté onion and garlic in margarine until soft.
3 Add tomatoes, basil, sugar, chopped capers, salt and pepper. Cook gently 10 min.
4 Stir in flour, then add wine and cook 5 min. Stir to prevent sticking.
5 Wash fish, dry and brush with PU oil.
6 Place half of tomato mixture in base of ovenproof dish, lay cutlets on top and cover with remaining mixture.

7 Cover with a piece of greased greaseproof paper.
8 Bake in preheated oven 375 or 5, 30 min. until fish is cooked.

Haddock is always recognisable by the black thumb mark on the skin towards the top of the fish.

Haddock in Mushroom Cream Sauce
1 lb. skinned fresh haddock fillet
2 oz. PU margarine
4 oz. button mushrooms
1 oz. flour
½ pint skimmed milk
Squeeze of garlic powder
Lemon juice
Salt and pepper
Pinch of mixed herbs
2 tbsps. natural low-fat yoghurt

1 Sprinkle the fish with salt, pepper and lemon juice
2 Melt the PU margarine in large frying pan.
3 Fry fish fillets 3 min. on each side.
4 Remove from pan and lay in base of shallow ovenproof dish.
5 Slice the mushrooms, add to remaining PU margarine in frying pan and sauté for 5 min.
6 Stir in the flour and add the milk gradually.
7 Slowly bring to boil to thicken, stirring all the time. Remove from heat.
8 Add mixed herbs, garlic powder and yoghurt to sauce, return to heat and cook for 1 min. very, very gently.
9 Pour over fish. Cover with greased greaseproof paper.
10 Bake 325 or 3; 30 min.

Cooking time may vary depending on the thickness of the fish.

Green Velvet Haddock
2 8-oz. fillets of fresh haddock
½ oz. PU margarine
Lemon juice
1 large packet frozen chopped spinach

1 tbsp. PU oil
2 level tbsps. plain flour
¼ pint skimmed milk
Salt and pepper

1 Wash fish and lay in shallow oven proof dish.
2 Sprinkle with lemon juice, salt and pepper and spread with margarine.
3 Cover with foil and bake 350 or 4, in centre of oven 20 min.
4 Blend PU oil, flour and skimmed milk in saucepan and bring slowly to boil stirring all the time.
5 Place block of spinach in pan with sauce, reduce heat as far as possible. Cover.
6 Frequently turn spinach over and scrape softened block into sauce until completely blended and thawed.
7 Season. Pour sauce over fish to completely cover.
8 Continue to bake for a further 15 min.

Use a fish slice to serve hot straight from the dish. Pommes Anna is a good choice of vegetable to accompany this recipe.

Scalloped Haddock Mornay

½ lb. fresh haddock fillet
½ oz. PU margarine
½ oz. flour
¼ pint skimmed milk
Salt and pepper
Lemon juice
1 slice carrot
1 slice onion
1 bay leaf
1 oz. grated cheddar cheese
Freshly mashed potato or 1¼ oz. instant dried potato (reconstituted).
Parsley for garnish

1 Poach fish gently in salted water and lemon juice to cover.
2 When fish is cooked, drain and flake. Remove any skin and bones.
3 Warm the milk in a pan with salt, pepper, onion, carrot and bay leaf.

4 Set aside to infuse (15 min.)
5 Prepare potato and fill a forcing bag with ½ in. star nozzle.
6 Melt PU margarine in small pan and stir in flour. Cook slightly.
7 Strain milk into another jug and then add gradually to the roux, stirring constantly.
8 Bring to the boil and allow to thicken.
9 Add half of grated cheese.
10 Add fish to the sauce and divide mixture between two scallop shells or individual dishes.
11 Pipe a border of potato around edges of shells.
12 Sprinkle grated cheese in centre and brown under the grill.
13 Garnish with a sprig of parsley.

Each serving of fish contains approx. 70 mg. cholesterol and the cheese content adds only a further 15 mg.

Smoked Haddock Mousse
1 smoked haddock (about 1 lb.)
2 level tbsps. chopped chives
1 5-oz. carton low fat yoghurt
2 level tbsps. cornflour
2 tbsps. skimmed milk
Cayenne

1 Place fish in large frying pan. Cover with cold water.
2 Bring to boil. Immediately lower heat and simmer 15 to 20 min. until cooked. Drain.
3 Remove skin and all bones.
4 Flake the fish and mix in chopped chives, cayenne and yoghurt.
5 Blend cornflour with cold skimmed milk.
6 Add to fish mixture and cook in saucepan over low heat until mixture thickens.

Serve as a starter with melba toast or with a green salad as a supper dish.
When poaching fish, the water should not be allowed to stay at boiling point as this may toughen the flesh.
Fish is cooked when it loses that 'glassy' look, and flesh is

opaque. The bones should come away easily when lifted with a fork, and a white fluid appears.

Orange Fish Fillets
1 lb. white fish fillets
Juice of 1 small onion
Juice of 1 orange
2 tbsps. PU oil
Salt and pepper

1 Season fillets with salt and pepper.
2 Place in shallow ovenproof dish.
3 Combine onion juice, orange juice and oil. Pour over fish.
4 Bake in oven 375 or 5. Approx. 30 min.

To obtain onion juice, grate an onion finely, and then pass through a small metal strainer, or pass small pieces through a garlic press.

Any white fish is suitable for this delicate supper dish. Choose from brill, cod, haddock, hake, halibut, plaice, sole or turbot.

Kedgeree
8 oz. long-grain rice
Small smoked haddock or 8 oz. smoked cod fillet
2 eggs
2 tbsps. PU oil
1 medium onion, chopped
1 tbsp. low-fat yoghurt
Paprika
Pepper

1 Cook rice in plenty of boiling salted water, drain and dry in usual way.
2 Poach fish in water, remove skin and bones. Flake flesh.
3 Boil eggs for 10 min., run under cold water and shell.
4 Cut through whites around centre and remove yolks (use yolks in sauce gribiche for those not following low cholesterol diet).
5 Sauté onion in oil until soft.
6 Add flaked fish, chopped egg whites and rice and stir until hot.

7 Add pepper, remove from heat.
8 Stir in yoghurt and turn on to serving dish.
9 Sprinkle with paprika. Serve hot.

No salt has been included in the seasoning, as smoked fish is usually quite salty.

Spicy Baked Herring
4 herrings
1 oz. PU margarine
1 level tbsp. horseradish sauce
2 level tbsps. tomato purée
3 tbsps. skimmed milk
3 level tbsps. fresh white breadcrumbs
Pinch sugar
Salt and pepper

1 Remove heads and gut and clean herrings.
2 Fillet herrings and discard roes.
3 Blend PU margarine, horseradish sauce, salt and pepper and spread over white flesh of fish.
4 Roll up each fish and place in a well fitting dish.
5 Stir tomato purée and sugar into milk and pour over fish.
6 Top with breadcrumbs and bake 350 or 4; 30 min.

Herrings are obtainable throughout the year but are at their best between July and March.

Braised Mackerel Superiore
½ pint dry white wine
1 onion
1 carrot
1 stick of celery
2 mackerel
1 bay leaf
10 peppercorns
Bouquet garni
Salt and pepper
2 oz. button mushrooms
2 tbsps. PU oil

1 Clean the mackerel and place in base of casserole.
2 Chop onion, carrot and celery and place in pan with wine, bay leaf, peppercorns, bouquet garni, salt and pepper.
3 Bring to boil, and then simmer 20 min. until reduced to half.
4 Strain liquor through a sieve over fish.
5 Cover and cook 20 min., 325 or 3.
6 Remove cover, baste and continue cooking until fish is soft and flaky, 20 to 30 min.
7 Sauté mushrooms in oil and use to garnish.
8 Serve hot or cold with lemon butterflies (see page 184).

Mackerel is obtainable at most times of the year and is highly nutritious. If you can bear to leave the roe for someone else to eat, do so; it does contain most of the cholesterol in this fish.

Plaice Asparagus Rolls

4 fillets plaice
1 small can asparagus tips
1 tbsp. PU oil
2 tbsps. plain flour
¼ tsp. salt
Liquor from asparagus made up to ½ pint with skimmed milk
Salt and pepper
2 tbsps. fried breadcrumbs

1 Skin plaice fillets and cut each into two, lengthways.
2 Season with salt and pepper.
3 Strain asparagus, keep liquor and make up to ½ pint with milk.
4 Place 2 asparagus tips across tail end of each fillet and roll up.
5 Put rolls in greased ovenproof dish to fit, so that they will not unroll.
6 Cover with foil and bake in oven, 350 or 4; 20 mins.
7 Blend liquor, oil, flour and salt in saucepan.
8 Bring to boil slowly and cook to thicken, stirring continuously.
9 Remove foil and pour sauce over fish.

10 Decorate with any remaining asparagus tips and sprinkle with breadcrumbs.
11 Raise heat to 400 or 6 and bake 10 mins.

Serve with potato nests filled with cooked mixed vegetables.

Fillets of Plaice Dugléré
1½ lb. plaice fillets
½ pint water
¼ pint white wine
4 bay leaves
1 small onion chopped
1 oz. PU margarine
1 oz. flour
1 tsp. chopped parsley
2 tomatoes, skinned and chopped
Salt and pepper
½ 5-oz. carton natural low-fat yoghurt

1 Skin the fish, sprinkle the fillets with salt and pepper, and lay in a greased oven proof dish. Pour the wine over the fillets.
2 Place the fish skins, bay leaves and onion in a saucepan with ½ pint water.
3 Bring to boil and simmer 15 min.
4 Remove skins and boil liquid rapidly until it is reduced to ¼ pint. Strain over fish.
5 Bake in a preheated oven 350 or 4, 15 minutes.
6 Remove fillets from liquor and keep warm.
7 Melt PU margarine in a saucepan. Stir in flour. Add the fish liquor and blend well. Bring to boil and cook for 2 min. stirring constantly. Adjust seasoning.
8 Stir in parsley and tomatoes.
9 Remove from heat, mix in yoghurt and pour over fish fillets.
10 Serve hot.

It is usual in the better fish recipes to remove the pips from the tomatoes. As the skins are also being discarded, this does not leave very much fruit and with the normal price of tomatoes would be most uneconomic. However, in the summer when they may be more plentiful and cheaper, it would be preferable to de-seed the tomatoes.

Grilled Salmon
2 thick fresh salmon steaks
1 tbsp. PU oil
Salt and pepper
Thin slices of peeled cucumber

1 Pre-heat grill.
2 Place oil, salt and pepper in shallow plate.
3 Rinse salmon in cold water, removing thick blood with salt.
4 Lay salmon in oil. Turn to coat the other side.
5 Remove salmon from plate and place on lined hot grill pan.
6 Grill about 7 min. each side until cooked.
7 Place on hot serving dish garnished with cucumber slices.

A piece of foil on grill pan will help to ease washing up. The salmon is cooked when light pressure with a fork separates the bone from the flesh.

Salmon Ring
1 ½-lb. can salmon
½ oz. gelatine
3 tbsps. water
½ pint skimmed milk
1½ oz. PU margarine
1½ oz. plain flour
1 tbsp. mayonnaise
Dash of worcestershire sauce
Seasoning
Cooked peas, diced cucumber and tomato

1 Open can of salmon, drain, remove large bones and black skin. Mash well.
2 Place gelatine in warm water and dissolve.
3 Melt PU margarine in pan, add flour and blend. Add milk, bring slowly to boil to thicken.
4 When cool add gelatine to sauce.

5 Add other ingredients and mix well.
6 Taste—adjust seasoning. Turn into ring mould.
7 Place in refrigerator for 2 hr.
8 Turn out.
9 Serve with green salad.

Agar-agar is a vegetable gelatine which may be used instead of the more usual animal gelatine, but the strength varies and it is best to follow the directions on the packet.

Half oz. animal gelatine sets 1 pint of liquid in cold weather. More must be used in hot weather.

Grilled Trout

1 (8-oz.) trout
2 tbsps. PU oil
1 tbsp. plain flour
Salt and pepper
Lemon wedge
½ tsp. chopped parsley
Dab of PU margarine

1 Prepare trout. Clean, remove entrails and eyes. Trim tail if necessary.
2 Gently draw sharp knife across fish two or three times to cut skin.
3 Mix flour with salt and pepper.
4 Dip fish in seasoned flour to coat.
5 Brush both sides with PU oil.
6 Grill 4 to 6 min. each side.
7 Serve with a dab of PU margarine. Garnish with lemon wedge and parsley.

Fresh or frozen trout are suitable. Rainbow trout are available throughout the year

A few split blanched almonds fried in 1 tbsp. of PU oil may be sprinkled on fish instead of parsley.

Tuna Stuffed Peppers

2 green peppers
1 medium onion
1 oz. PU margarine

1 small can tuna fish
4 oz. boiled rice
Dash worcestershire sauce
A little water

1 Remove top and seeds from peppers.
2 Blanche in boiling water, 2 min.
3 Remove from saucepan and drain well.
4 Chop the onion and fry gently in ½ oz. PU margarine.
5 Drain tuna fish and flake the flesh.
6 Add fish, rice, salt, pepper and worcestershire sauce to the onions in the pan. Bind together.
7 Fill the peppers with this stuffing and stand in a greased ovenproof dish which is just large enough to prevent the peppers from falling.
8 Pour a little water into base of dish to reach about ½ in. up sides.
9 Dab remaining butter on top of the peppers.
10 Bake in oven, 350 or 4; 15 min.

Use grapefruit knife to remove the cores from the peppers. Peppers are very rich in Vitamin C.

7. Poultry

Chicken Bake

4 chicken portions
2 oz. fresh white breadcrumbs
½ oz. parmesan cheese
3 tbsps. PU oil
1 small onion, finely chopped
Salt and pepper

1 Fry onion in PU oil until golden brown.
2 Add breadcrumbs and fry until oil is absorbed but crumbs are not coloured.
3 Remove skin from chicken portions.
4 Rub salt and pepper over chicken and arrange in shallow ovenproof dish
5 Spread crumb mixture carefully over upper side of chicken pieces.
6 Sprinkle with cheese.
7 Bake in preheated oven, 350 or 4, 1 to 1½ hr. depending on thickness of portions.

Chicken Chasseur

Per person:
1 chicken quarter
2 tbsps. PU oil
1 small onion
2 oz. mushrooms
Garlic to taste
2 tomatoes

2 tbsps. dry white wine
1 tbsp. brandy
2 tbsps. water
Salt, pepper and pinch tarragon

1 Chop onion and mushrooms. Skin and chop tomatoes.
  Crush garlic if using fresh.
2 Wash and clean chicken. Remove skin.
3 Melt oil in pan and brown chicken all over.
4 Remove chicken from pan and set aside.
5 Add onion to pan and fry until fawn colour.
6 Add mushrooms, tomatoes and garlic and cook for a few
  moments.
7 Return chicken to pan and raise heat.
8 Pour on brandy and flambé.
9 Add wine, water, seasonings and tarragon.
10 Cover and cook until chicken is tender and sauce syrupy,
   30 min.

Serve in a hot dish surrounded with croûtes of fried
bread.

The skin of chicken is said to contain more cholesterol
than the flesh, but can be used for preparing stock provided
all fat is later removed.

Chicken 'n' Chips

4 chicken joints
2 level tsps. paprika
$\frac{1}{2}$ level tsp. ground ginger
Pinch of garlic powder
Salt and pepper
2 tbsps. PU oil
$\frac{1}{4}$ pint water
1$\frac{1}{2}$ lb. peeled chipped potatoes

1 Wash, clean and skin chicken joints.
2 Dry on kitchen paper.
3 Mix paprika, ground ginger, garlic powder, salt and pepper together.
4 Rub mixture using fingertips over all surfaces of chicken.
5 Brush with oil.
6 Pour water into roasting tin, place chicken pieces on rack.

7 Bake 375 or 5, approx. 1 hr. Baste occasionally to avoid drying out.
8 Peel and chip potatoes and deep fat fry 375°F (see under chipped potatoes, page 183).
9 Drain chicken and chips and serve in a basket or wooden bowl lined with white paper serviettes.

As a rule allow 8 oz. unprepared potato per person but taking into acount the fact that 6 chips are 100 calories it might be better to fry a few less, thus helping to resist temptation.

Chicken Croquettes

8 oz. minced cooked chicken
¼ pint de-fatted chicken stock
1 oz. PU margarine
1 oz. plain flour
1 tsp. soya flour
1 egg white
1 tsp. lemon juice
Salt and pepper
Fresh white breadcrumbs

1 Melt PU margarine in pan. Stir in flour and soya flour.
2 Gradually add chicken stock and bring to boil to thicken.
3 Remove from heat and add chicken, lemon juice, salt and pepper.
4 Bind with egg white (mixture should be moist).
5 Form into croquettes and coat with breadcrumbs.
6 Press crumbs in well with palette knife.
7 Fry in deep PU oil 375°F until golden brown.

If mixture is too dry, breadcrumbs will not adhere. Beat up another egg white and coat croquettes with this. Follow with a further covering of crumbs.

Chicken Orange Casserole

1 3½ lb. chicken
Juice of 3 large oranges
¼ pint of chicken stock

2 oz. flaked almonds
2 oz. white grapes (de-pipped)
1 oz. cornflour
Salt and pepper
Water

1 Skin and joint the chicken and divide into eight pieces. Place in large casserole.
2 Squeeze the oranges and pour over chicken. Add stock salt and pepper.
3 Cover casserole and cook in oven 325 or 3, 1½ to 2 hr. Baste occasionally.
4 Blend cornflour with a little cold water.
5 Add to casserole and blend.
6 Cut grapes in half, turn onto chicken, and sprinkle with flaked almonds.
7 Replace lid. Raise heat to 375 or 5 and cook for a further 20 min.

Chicken Oriental
1 3 lb. chicken
1 wine glass sweet sherry
1 wine glass soya sauce
1 tsp. ground ginger
1 lb. large green peppers
3 tbsps. PU oil
Salt and pepper
2 level tsps. cornflour

1 Remove skin and bone from chicken.
2 Cut flesh into chunks.
3 Combine sherry, soya sauce, ginger, salt and pepper.
4 Marinate chicken in this mixture for 1 hr. Turn occasionally.
5 Wash and de-seed green peppers. Cut into 1 in. squares.
6 Remove chicken from marinade. Quickly fry in PU oil until brown.
7 Add green peppers, lower heat and cover tightly.
8 Simmer 30 min. or until chicken is tender.
9 Blend cornflour with remainder of marinade, place in a saucepan and bring to boil. Pour into heated jug.

Serve chicken on a bed of hot boiled rice. Hand sauce separately.

It may be easier to cut the chicken into quarters before removing the skin and flesh.

Chicken Suprême
1 chicken, jointed and cleaned
1 quartered onion
1 sliced carrot
1 bay leaf
Salt and pepper
2 tbsps. PU oil
3 tbsps. plain flour
½ pint chicken stock

1 Simmer chicken in pan with salt, pepper, bay leaf, onion and carrot, and water to cover. Cover with lid.
2 Cook until tender, topping up with boiling water as necessary. 30 min. approx.
3 Strain the liquor and set it aside in a cold place for the fat to rise to the top.
4 Remove bones and skin from the chicken and cut flesh into bite-sized pieces.
5 When stock is cold, remove all fat.
6 Blend oil and flour in a saucepan and slowly add ½ pint chicken stock. Slowly bring to boil to thicken.
7 Add chicken pieces to sauce, adjust seasoning and add more stock if necessary.
8 Heat thoroughly and serve on bed of boiled rice.

The best way to remove the fat is to set the stock aside and, when cool enough, put it in the refrigerator overnight, when it will be easy to lift off the entire covering of fat.

A crisp green side salad completes the dish.

Chicken and Sweet Corn Pie
8 oz. plain flour
4 oz. PU margarine (hardened in freezer for 1 hr. if possible)
3 tbsps. skimmed milk
Pinch salt
2 cooked chicken quarters
1 onion

2 tbsps. sweet corn
1 slice lean ham
Pepper
1 egg white

1 Sieve flour and salt into mixing bowl.
2 Rub in PU margarine lightly.
3 Mix to a smooth dough with skimmed milk.
4 Roll out half the pastry dough and cut four rounds to fit bases of individual pie dishes.
5 Place in refrigerator. Put remaining dough in polythene bag and refrigerate.
6 Dice chicken, finely chop onion and ham and mix with sweet corn.
7 Add pepper and bind with egg white.
8 Remove pastry from refrigerator. Fill lined dishes with mixture.
9 Roll remaining pastry dough and cut out rounds for lids.
10 Damp edges of pie bases, place pastry lids over filling and seal well.
11 Mark with a fork, knock up edges and brush with skimmed milk.
12 Bake in a pre-heated oven, 400 or 6. Approx. 30 min.

Foil dishes are useful for individual servings.

These pies may be stored in a freezer before baking. It will then be necessary to allow an extra 15 min. cooking time.

Chicken Walnut Risotto
1 onion
2 oz. mushrooms
4 oz. long-grain rice
2 oz. PU margarine (approx.)
$\frac{3}{4}$ pint chicken stock
Pinch saffron
Salt and pepper
2 oz. walnuts (previously soaked)
4 oz. cooked chicken

1 Chop onion and slice mushrooms.
2 Fry in 1 oz. PU margarine until light brown, 5 min.

3 Wash and drain rice and add to pan.
4 Lower heat and stir until margarine is absorbed. (Add more margarine if necessary.)
5 Dissolve saffron in hot stock and add to mixture. Season well.
6 Chop walnuts and chicken and add to mixture.
7 Cover pan tightly and simmer until all liquid has been absorbed.

Keep hot in a covered casserole in oven 300 or 2.

If you use fresh walnuts they need no soaking. Packaged walnut halves or pieces should be covered with boiling water and left to soak 30 min. Drain and cover with cold water. Leave to soak 2 hr. Rinse and use. The pungent, slightly bitter, flavour of the nuts will have disappeared.

Remember that of all the nuts, walnuts have the most value in a cholesterol-controlled diet.

Galantine of Chicken
1 4–5 lb.-chicken
1 onion, quartered
1 bay leaf
6 oz. cooked ham
2 truffles or pickled walnuts
½ oz. skinned pistachio nuts
12 oz. lean minced pork
1 tsp. finely chopped parsley
Salt and pepper
1 wine glass madeira
Stock to cover galantine while cooking
¾ pint béchamel sauce
¼ oz. gelatine

1 Bone uncooked chicken, taking care not to cut skin unnecessarily.
2 Chop pickled walnuts and pistachio nuts.
3 Shred ham.
4 Open out the boned chicken, the skin on the underside.
5 Mix pork, chopped parsley and madeira together. Season.
6 Spread half the mixture over centre panel of chicken.
7 Cover with a layer of ham, walnuts and pistachios.

8 Cover with remaining pork mixture.
9 Fold two long edges to centre, then fold two short edges to centre. Make sure stuffing is inside.
10 Stitch with trussing needle and string.
11 Wrap tightly in a piece of muslin or foil.
12 Place in large saucepan or pressure cooker.
13 Cover with stock, add bay leaf and onion. Cook in saucepan 2 to 3 hr., turning once, or in pressure cooker at 15 lb. pressure 45 min.
14 When cooked wrap in clean piece of muslin and press between two boards, or trays, with a 4 lb. weight on top.

When cool transfer to refrigerator: 24 hr. later remove cloth and string. Decorate with ¾ pint (15 fl. oz.) béchamel sauce thickened with ¼ oz. gelatine.

Serve cold, sliced with a green salad.

When chicken has been boned the flesh will weigh two thirds original weight.

Chicken Sauté with Walnuts

2 oz. shelled walnuts
2 tbsps. PU oil
4 chicken joints
1 small onion
¼ pint dry white wine
¼ pint water
Salt and pepper
Cornflour for coating

1 Finely chop onion.
2 Place oil in frying pan and lightly fry walnuts. Switch off heat, remove and drain walnuts. Leave oil in pan.
3 Wash and clean chicken portions and remove skin.
4 Season chicken and coat with cornflour.
5 Fry chicken pieces and chopped onion until golden brown.
6 Add wine and water. Cover and simmer gently 20 min. or until chicken is cooked.
7 Return nuts to pan, lift chicken on to serving dish and cover with sauce.

Serve with rice and green salad.

Suprême de Volaille
4 Chicken breasts
4 tbsps. fresh white breadcrumbs
Juice and rind of ½ lemon
Salt and pepper
2 egg whites
3 tbsps. PU oil

1 Slice flesh away from bone. Retain bone and any skin for making stock.
2 Lightly beat egg white with lemon juice.
3 Mix breadcrumbs with lemon rind.
4 Season chicken breasts. Dip in egg mixture and breadcrumbs, twice. Press crumbs in with palette knife.
5 Fry in PU oil 10 min., turning once. Add more oil if necessary.

A white sauce based on chicken stock and flavoured with with anchovy essence may be served separately.

Turkey Lombardia
4 oz. plain noodles
8 oz. cooked turkey
2 oz. walnuts, chopped
4 oz. mushrooms, sliced
1 oz. PU margarine
1 oz. plain flour
1 pint chicken stock
1 small onion, chopped
2 oz. grated parmesan cheese
Salt and pepper
2 tbsps. PU oil

1 Cook the noodles in boiling salted water until tender. Drain.
2 Sauté mushrooms, onions and walnuts in PU oil, 3 min.
3 Melt PU margarine in saucepan over gentle heat, stir in flour and gradually whisk in chicken stock. Bring to boil to thicken. Season.
4 Switch off heat. Stir in noodles and drained mushrooms, onions and walnuts.
5 Chop turkey roughly, add to mixture then turn into an ovenproof casserole.

6 Sprinkle cheese evenly over top.
7 Bake in a preheated oven, 375 or 5, until golden brown.
8 Serve hot.

Chicken, tuna fish or salmon may be used in place of turkey.

Turkey and Melon Salad
8 oz. cooked turkey
1 green pepper
1 ogen or charentais melon
2 oz. shelled walnuts
2 tbsps. PU mayonnaise
A few sprigs of parsley for garnish

1 Cut melon in half and remove seeds.
2 Scoop out flesh with melon baller or teaspoon.
3 De-seed and chop pepper and walnuts. Cut turkey into chunks.
4 Combine all ingredients, taking care not to squash melon balls.
5 Pile into melon shells and garnish with parsley.

Vary the recipe by using chicken or ham in place of turkey.
One tbsp. mayonnaise made with egg yolk would give 8 mg. cholesterol.

Beef Olives

1 lb. braising steak (or small joint topside of beef)
2 oz. fresh breadcrumbs
1 oz. PU margarine
1 tbsp. finely chopped parsley
1 level tsp. mixed dried herbs
Grated rind of 1 lemon
Skimmed milk to bind
Salt and pepper.

Sauce
1 tbsp. PU oil
½ oz. plain flour
½ pint stock
1 small carrot
1 small onion
Salt and pepper

1 Remove all fat from meat.
2 Slice meat thinly and flatten with a meat batter or rolling pin.
3 Cut meat into 4 in. squares.
4 Mix breadcrumbs, PU margarine, parsley, herbs, lemon rind, salt and pepper with sufficient milk to bind.
5 Place stuffing down centre of each piece of meat.
6 Roll up and tie with string. Set aside.
7 Prepare sauce. Peel and slice carrot and onion and fry in PU oil until brown.
8 Add the flour and stir. Cook slowly until flour is light brown and a nutty flavour.

9 Add stock and seasoning and stir until mixture boils and thickens.
10 Lay beef olives in sauce in frying pan. Cover with well fitting lid or aluminium foil and simmer 2 hr. until beef is tender. Add more water if necessary.
11 Remove string from meat.
12 Pile beef olives in centre of serving dish and strain sauce over. Discard carrot and onion.

Garnish with petits pois and piped potato.

Cabbage Dolmas

A few outside leaves of a green cabbage
4 oz. fresh minced beef (lean only)
1 egg white (from large egg)
1 tbsp. skimmed milk
1 slice wholemeal bread
2 tsps. tomato purée
½ oz. PU margarine
Salt and pepper

1 Blanche cabbage leaves, remove hard stem and drain on kitchen paper.
2 Remove crusts from bread.
3 Beat egg white gently, add milk and season with salt and pepper.
4 Mash bread into egg.
5 Fry meat in PU margarine. Add tomato purée.
6 Add meat to egg mixture.
7 If mixture is not stiff enough, add some more crumbled bread.
8 Place a spoonful of stuffing on each leaf and form into parcels.
9 Place in a well-fitting greased ovenproof dish, folded edges underneath.
10 Place a dab of PU margarine on top
11 Cover with lid or foil. Bake 375 or 5; 15 to 20 min.
12 Bake in centre of oven if possible.
13 When cooked, coat with brown piquant sauce (see page 116).

A very economical meat dish, which is reminiscent of the Greek dolmas (stuffed vine leaves).

Substitute 2 oz. of the meat with soya protein minced beef substitute, obtainable at health food shops. Follow the directions on the packet as these vary. Usually soya minced beef is added dry to stews, or soaked in water for use in patties, rissoles, etc.

Cannelloni

3–4 oz. cannelloni (in tube form)
1 tsp. PU oil

Filling
1 small onion
½ pint water or stock
1 tbsp. PU oil
12 oz. minced lean beef
2 oz. round rice
2 level tsps. chopped parsley
½ level tsp. salt
¼ level tsp. pepper
1 tbsp. lemon juice

Topping
½ pint espagnole sauce (page 117). *or*
½ pint béchemel sauce (page 115).

1 Peel and finely chop onion.
2 Heat 1 tbsp. PU oil in saucepan and gently fry onion for a few minutes.
3 Add minced beef and toss in oil until brown.
4 Stir in rice, parsley, salt and pepper. Cook 2 min.
5 Add stock and lemon juice. Bring to boil and simmer covered for 20 min. until all stock has been absorbed and minced beef is cooked.
6 Drop pieces of cannelloni one at a time into a large pan of boiling salted water to which 1 tsp. PU oil has been added.
7 Simmer 12 min. until cannelloni is firm but tender. Drain in colander and rinse under cold running water.
8 Fill each piece of pasta with a little mince mixture and arrange in ovenproof dish.
9 Coat with sauce.
10 Bake 375 or 5; 25 to 30 min. until hot.

Cannelloni, which is a type of pasta, may be purchased in square or tubular shapes or may be prepared at home from flour, water and oil. The round rice used for puddings is more gelatinous than long grain rice and more suitable in this recipe.

Casserole of Beef in Brown Ale

1 lb. lean stewing steak
2 large onions (sliced)
Bouquet garni
3 tbsps. PU oil
½ pint brown ale
2 level tbsps. plain flour
Squeeze of garlic powder
4 oz. mushrooms
Salt and pepper

1 Tenderize the meat with a cleaver or rolling pin.
2 Cut meat into 1 in. cubes.
3 Put oil in pan, bring to high temperature and toss meat in. Stir rapidly to seal and brown.
4 Add onions and fry gently.
5 Stir in flour.
6 Add brown ale and bring to boil to thicken.
7 Discard mushroom stalks, roughly chop caps and add to pan.
8 Season, add bouqet garni and turn into ovenproof casserole.
9 Cover tightly and cook in oven. 325 or 3; 2 hr.

Check once or twice during cooking to be sure that liquor is not drying up too much. If this happens, add a few tbsps. boiling water.

Dishes cooked with beer do not reveal their true flavour until dish is finally cooked. Tasting during cooking may produce a bitter flavour which will disappear on completion. Be sure to remove bouquet garni before serving.

Caucasian Hot pot

1 lb. lean stewing beef
½ lb. potatoes
½ lb. carrots
½ lb. tomatoes
8 cabbage leaves

1 oz. plain flour
Salt and pepper
1 tsp. carraway seeds
2 tbsps. PU oil
¼ pint vegetable stock

1 Peel and slice potatoes. (Keep in cold water, drain when required.)
2 Scrape and slice carrots.
3 Skin tomatoes and slice thickly.
4 Wash cabbage leaves in cold water.
5 Cut meat into 1 in. cubes.
6 Toss in seasoned flour.
7 Place PU oil in pan and quickly fry meat until sealed and brown. Stir constantly. Add carraway seeds.
8 Place layers of potatoes, meat, carrots, cabbage and tomatoes in large casserole.
9 Pour in stock and cover with well fitting lid.
10 Cook 350 or 4; 2 to 2½ hr. Add more stock if necessary, and adjust seasoning half way through cooking time.

A complete dinner in one casserole.

Curry House Curry

1 lb. cubed uncooked beef or lamb or one chicken cut into eight pieces
3 tbsps. PU oil
1 large onion, finely chopped
1 tbsp. tomato purée
1 tbsp. curry powder (garam masala)
1 clove of garlic (crushed)
2 tsps. rice flour (or ground rice)
Squeeze of lemon juice
½ pint stock
Salt to taste

1 Fry onion and garlic in PU oil for 4 or 5 min. until onion begins to turn colour.
2 Stir in curry powder and rice flour, and fry 2 min.
3 Toss in cubed meat or chicken, and stir to seal and *brown* all surfaces.
4 Stir tomato purée and stock into meat and add salt to taste.

5 Bring to boil, cover and lower heat to simmering point.
6 Cook until tender, about 1½ hr. Add a squeeze of lemon juice.

If the gravy is too thin, remove the lid from the saucepan and boil rapidly for a few minutes.

Serve with boiled rice (see page 64), dhal (see page 53) and chapatis.

To make chapatis mix 2 or 3 heaped tbsps. atta or wholemeal flour with sufficient cold water to form a soft paste. Cover and rest for at least 30 min. Then, using plenty of flour, divide into small pieces and roll out to the size of a pancake. Cook for 1 or 2 min. each side in a dry frying pan or under the grill.

Hamburger Balls in Rich Red Wine Sauce

1 lb. home minced lean beef
1 medium onion
1 medium potato (6 oz.)
1 tsp. beef extract
Salt and pepper
¾ pint rich red wine sauce

1 Light oven, 350 or 4.
2 Peel and finely grate onion.
3 Peel and finely grate potato.
4 Blend minced beef, onion, potato, salt and pepper and beef extract.
5 Form into walnut-sized balls and place in ovenproof dish.
6 Bake uncovered 20 min.
7 Pour sauce over meat balls and continue cooking covered for a further 30 min.

Sauce
1 oz. PU margarine
1 oz. plain flour
1 ½-pint can beef consommé
½ pint water
1 carrot
1 small onion
1 bay leaf
1 level tbsp. tomato purée
3 tbsps. red wine
Salt and pepper

1 Peel and finely slice carrot and onion.
2 Melt PU margarine in saucepan and sauté carrot and onion slowly until golden brown.
3 Stir in flour and continue cooking until flour is brown (but not burnt). Stir continuously.
4 Gradually add consommé and water. Stir well and bring to boil.
5 Reduce heat to simmer, add bay leaf, tomato purée and seasoning.
6 Cook as slowly as possible until sauce is reduced by one third.
7 Press through sieve. Discard pulp.
8 Stir in red wine and cook a further 10 min.
9 Use as directed above.

The slower the sauce is cooked, the better the flavour will be.

Nearly Beef Stroganoff

1 lb. lean fillet of beef
6 oz. onions peeled and chopped
2 oz. PU margarine
8 oz. mushrooms, washed and sliced
¼ pint canned consommé
1 5-oz. carton low-fat yoghurt
1 tsp. cornflour
1 tbsp. chopped parsley
Salt and pepper

1 Cut beef into strips 2 in. × ¼ in. × ¼ in.
2 Fry beef strips in PU margarine over high heat stirring constantly to prevent sticking and burning.
3 Add onions and continue frying at a slightly lower temperature until meat is brown.
4 Add consommé and mushrooms and simmer until meat becomes tender. Season.
5 Stir cornflour into yoghurt and add to meat. Bring to boil and remove from heat at once.
6 Sprinkle with parsley and serve hot on bed of boiled rice.

Cheap quality frying steak may be substituted if beaten well to tenderize.

Our Favourite Braised Beef

1 lb. good quality braising steak
2 large onions
1 large carrot
2 bay leaves
1 tbsp. beef or yeast extract
Salt and pepper
Boiling water

1 Trim all surplus fat from meat and discard.
2 Cut steak into ¾ in. thick pieces about 2 in. square.
3 Place in bottom of large casserole.
4 Peel and slice onions and carrot.
5 Tip onto steak.
6 Place bay leaves on top.
7 Dissolve beef in ½ pint boiling water.
8 Season to taste.
9 Pour liquid into casserole adding more water to completely cover the meat.
10 Place tightly fitting lid on casserole.
11 Cook in oven 300 or 2; 4 hr.

Ideal for the working wife. This dish may be cooked at a lower temperature, viz. 250 to 275 or ½ to 1, for 7 to 8 hr.

For non-slimmers supply plenty of fresh bread to soak up the delicious gravy.

Savoury Mince Pancakes

½ pint pancake batter
¼ lb. fresh lean minced beef
1 small onion
1 tsp. tomato ketchup
½ oz. PU margarine
1 tomato
Salt and pepper
½ oz. flour
3 tbsps. water
1 tsp. beef or yeast extract
½ pint tomato sauce (see page 118)

1 Make pancakes and set aside by tacking between pieces of greased greaseproof paper.

2 Chop onion.
3 Skin tomato and chop coarsely.
4 Heat PU margarine and fry onion.
5 Add minced beef and tomato. Stir and brown lightly.
6 Add tomato ketchup, salt and pepper.
7 Stir in flour ($\frac{1}{2}$ level tbsp.).
8 Add water and beef or yeast extract. Stir, cover and leave to simmer until meat is cooked. Stir occasionally.
9 Divide mixture between pancakes, roll up and pour hot tomato sauce over them.
10 Place in a moderate oven, 375 or 5. Cover and heat through, 10 min.

Special Occasion Fillet Steak
2 fillet steaks
1 small onion
4 oz. mushrooms
2 medium thick slices white bread
$\frac{1}{4}$ pint red wine
$\frac{1}{4}$ pint water
$\frac{1}{2}$ oz. cornflour
2 tbsps. PU oil
Salt and pepper

1 Remove crusts from bread and cut to the same size as the steaks.
2 Fry slices of bread until crisp and light brown.
3 Peel and slice onion and fry until brown. Add more oil if necessary.
4 Peel and slice mushrooms and add to onions. Season.
5 Add wine and cook 5 min.
6 Blend cornflour with cold water and add to pan. Stir. Bring to boil to thicken.
7 Fry steaks quickly on either side and lower heat until cooked to taste.
8 Place each steak on fried bread and cover with sauce.

A 1 in. thick steak requires 8 to 15 min. to cook.

Steak Pie

1 lb. buttock steak
2 tbsps. flour
4 oz. mushrooms
Water
Salt and pepper

Pastry
4 oz. plain flour
4 tbsps. PU oil
2 tbsps. cold milk
Pinch salt

1 Wipe steak and cut into 1 in. cubes.
2 Mix flour with salt and pepper. Coat meat cubes in this seasoned flour.
3 Place meat in casserole.
4 Wash and slice mushrooms. Add to casserole.
5 Cover with water.
6 Place lid on casserole and cook in oven, 300 or 2, 2½ hr.
7 Transfer meat to cold pie dish. Dampen edge of dish. Add 4 or 5 tbsps. of the gravy. Reserve remainder of gravy.
8 Sieve flour and salt into mixing bowl.
9 Combine oil and milk. Add to flour and mix to a soft dough.
10 Roll paste between two sheets of greaseproof paper to measurements of pie dish.
11 Remove top sheet of greaseproof paper, and turn paste on to steak with underside paper. Discard paper.
12 Mark edges with fork to seal paste onto dish.
13 Raise oven temperature to 450 or 8.
14 Bake pie 15 min. Lower heat to 350 or 4, and bake for a further 20 min.
15 Serve with remaining gravy.

If the meat is more fatty than you would wish, rapidly cool after initial casseroling, then freeze until fat solidifies on surface. Remove fat, thaw and continue recipe at stage 11.

Sukiyaki

1 lb. lean frying steak
8 oz. vermicelli
4 oz. mushrooms

1 stick of celery
½ bunch spring onions
2 leeks
Small can bamboo shoots
3 tbsps. PU oil

Sauce
½ pint water
½ tsp. monosodium glutamate
1 wine glass soya sauce
1 wine glass sweet sherry
1 level tbsp. caster sugar

1 Cook vermicelli in boiling salted water until just tender. Drain.
2 Slice meat and vegetables thinly.
3 Fry meat quickly in PU oil. Remove from pan and drain.
4 Toss vegetables in the oil remaining in the frying pan.
5 Add sauce ingredients and bring to boil.
6 Place vermicelli in serving dish, pour vegetables and sauce over and arrange meat on top.

A modified version of a popular Japanese dish, the vegetables should be crunchy and the meat only just cooked.

Boiled Leg of Lamb with Caper Sauce
2½ lb. joint leg of lamb (top half)
Bouquet garni
2 carrots (peeled and quartered)
1 onion (peeled and quartered)
2 tsps. salt
Water
Caper sauce

1 Wipe meat with damp cloth and remove all visible fat.
2 Weigh joint to calculate cooking time. Allow 20 min. per pound and 20 min. over.
3 Place meat in large saucepan with bouquet garni, carrots, onions and salt.
4 Add cold water to just cover.
5 Bring to boil. Boil rapidly for 5 min. to seal the outside.
6 Turn down heat and simmer, covered for required time. (In this case a minimum of 1 hr. 10 min.)

7 When cooked, drain. Discard herbs and vegetables. Rinse
  in fresh boiling water to remove any fat adhering to joint.
8 Place on serving dish and coat with caper sauce.

Suitable vegetables to serve with this dish are sliced carrots
and turnips.

Cotelettes au Jambon

4 cutlets from best end neck of lamb
2 oz. lean cooked ham or 2 tbsps. smokey bacon flavour
  soya protein
3 tbsps. fresh white breadcrumbs
2 egg whites
3 tbsps. PU oil
Duchesse potatoes
Salt and pepper

1 Trim cutlets removing as much fat as possible.
2 Chop ham.
3 Mix breadcrumbs with ham or smokey bacon soya
  protein.
4 Beat egg whites lightly with salt and pepper.
5 Dip cutlets in beaten egg white.
6 Coat with mixed crumbs—press in well with palette
  knife.
7 Heat oil in frying pan and fry cutlets 10–12 min., turning
  once.
8 Pipe potato on centre of dish and stand cutlets upright
  one behind the other.
9 Serve with a piquant brown sauce separately.

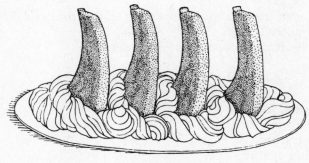

Cotelettes au jambon

Textured soya protein food is available at nearly all health food shops and costs about half the price of animal meats. If used in this recipe 40 mg. cholesterol would be saved.

Lamb Louise

1 piece of best end neck of lamb (five or six bones)
1 aubergine
½ lb. courgettes
1 cucumber
1 large onion
4 tomatoes
1 clove garlic
Salt and pepper
Sprig of thyme
1 bay leaf
1 tbsp. freshly chopped parsley
3 tbsps. PU oil

1 Wipe joint of lamb with damp cloth. Remove surplus fat.
2 Place on a wire rack in baking tin. Roast in a preheated oven, 400 or 6. Approx. 35 min.
3 Peel aubergine, courgettes, cucumber and tomatoes. Cut into thick slices.
4 Peel and chop onion and crush garlic.
5 Fry onion and garlic in PU oil, 5 min.
6 Add prepared vegetables, thyme, bay leaf and seasoning.
7 Lower heat, cover with lid and cook gently until soft. Stir occasionally.
8 Drain lamb on absorbent paper. Cut into five or six cutlets.
9 Place vegetable mixture on hot serving dish, and arrange cutlets on top.
10 Sprinkle chopped parsley over meat.

Serve boiled rice as an accompaniment.

Lamb Navarin

2 carrots
1 large onion
1 lb. potatoes
Garlic powder

1½ lb. leg of lamb
2 level tbsps. flour
2 tbsps. PU oil
1 level tbsp. beef extract
1 pint water
1 level tbsp. tomato puree
3 bay leaves
½ level tsp. mixed dried herbs
Pinch sugar
Salt and pepper

1 Remove skin and fat from lamb and cut flesh away from bone.
2 Cut meat into 1 in. cubes.
3 Combine flour, salt, pepper and mixed dried herbs in a large polythene bag.
4 Drop the lamb cubes into the bag and shake well to coat.
5 Heat oil in saucepan and fry meat until light brown.
6 Peel and slice carrots and onion and add to pan with squeeze of garlic powder. Lower heat and cook 5 min.
7 Stir in extract, water, tomato purée and sugar.
8 Bring to boil.
9 Peel and cut potatoes into chunks. Place in casserole. Add bay leaves.
10 Pour meat mixture on top.
11 Cover casserole with lid and place in centre of oven.
12 Cook 350 or 4, 1½ hr. Adjust seasoning.

Remove bay leaves when serving.
Navarin is a complete hot winter supper and need not be accompanied by additional vegetables.

Lamb Sweet and Sour Kebabs
1 lb. lean lamb (leg of lamb is suitable)
8 oz. can pineapple chunks
1 Green pepper
1 Red pepper
4 oz. button mushrooms
8 pearl onions (pickled onions)
8 bay leaves
2 tbsps. clear honey

2 tbsps. malt vinegar
2 level tbsps. soft brown sugar
Pinch dried herbs
Salt and pepper

1 Drain pineapple and reserve juice.
2 Cut lamb into 1 in. cubes.
3 Drop peppers into boiling water and blanch 2 min.
4 Drain peppers. Core and de-seed.
5 Wipe mushrooms and cut off bottoms of stalks.
6 Thread lamb, peppers, mushrooms, onions, pineapple and bay leaves on kebab skewers.
7 Blend honey, vinegar, sugar, pineapple juice, salt and pepper and herbs in small pan and stir until sugar is dissolved. Bring to boil.
8 Heat grill, coat kebabs with sauce and place filled skewers on grill.
9 Cook about 12 min. turning frequently and spoon a little more sauce over kebabs every few minutes.

Remove kebabs from skewers with a fork and serve hot on a bed of rice.

Moussaka
2 large aubergines
1 onion, finely chopped
1 lb. lean minced lamb or beef
2 tomatoes, skinned and chopped
2 tbsps. tomato purée
3 tbsps. chopped parsley
½ pint béchamel sauce (page 115)
Salt and pepper
PU oil
1 tbsp. flour
½ clove garlic, crushed
¼ tsp. cinnamon
2 tbsps. water

1 Peel aubergines and slice thinly. Place in colander, sprinkle with salt and leave 30 min.
2 Rinse in cold water. Dry on absorbent kitchen paper.
3 Dredge lightly with flour and fry gently in PU oil.

4 Drain.
5 Fry onion and garlic in the same frying pan in PU oil (2 tbsps.).
6 Add minced meat. Fry until brown.
7 Stir in tomatoes, tomato purée, parsley, cinnamon, salt, pepper and water. Simmer 15 min.
8 Arrange layers of aubergine and meat mixture in deep ovenproof dish, finishing with aubergine slices.
9 Pour béchamel sauce over meat mixture.
10 Bake in preheated oven, 350 or 4. Approx. 45 min. until brown on top.

Boiled sliced potatoes may be substituted for aubergines. An egg yolk added to the béchamel sauce will improve the moussaka.

Baked Gammon Rolls
8 thinly sliced gammon rashers
1 small can pineapple tidbits or pieces
4 tbsps. fresh white breadcrumbs
1 egg white
Freshly ground black pepper
2 tbsps. dry white wine or cider
2 tbsps. PU oil

1 Drain pineapple.
2 Mix with breadcrumbs and pepper and bind with lightly beaten egg white.
3 Trim all fat from gammon rashers.
4 Spread each rasher with pineapple stuffing.
5 Roll up and tie securely with cotton.
6 Brown quickly in oil.
7 Remove from frying pan and transfer to casserole.
8 Pour wine over gammon rolls. Cover.
9 Bake 375 or 5, 25 min.

If you prefer a sweeter dish, mix a little pineapple syrup with the wine.

Pork Chops with Apricot Stuffing
4 thick pork chops (preferably chump)
2 tbsps. flour
3 oz. dried apricots

½ oz. PU margarine
1 level tbsp. finely chopped onion
1½ oz. fresh white breadcrumbs
2 tsps. lemon juice
½ level tsp. dried rosemary
½ level tsp. mustard powder
Salt and pepper

1 Cover apricots with cold water. Bring to boil and simmer 5 min.
2 Drain. Chop apricots roughly.
3 Fry onion in PU margarine until soft.
4 Remove pan from heat and stir in apricots, breadcrumbs, lemon juice, rosemary, mustard, salt and pepper to taste. Mixture should be fairly stiff.
5 Trim all fat from chops and cut horizontally through centre of chop towards bone to form an opening. Do not cut chop completely in half.

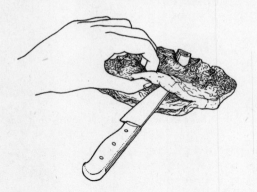

Stuffing pork chops

6 Divide stuffing into four and fill centre pocket. Press well in. Shape and secure with wooden cocktail sticks.
7 Dredge with flour and grill quickly under fierce heat, 3 to 4 min. each side.
8 Transfer to ovenproof dish and bake, 350 or 4, 45 min.

Pork when well trimmed contains no more cholesterol than lamb or beef. The chops tend to be larger so that the daily meat allowance must be considered.

Spit Roast Pork with Apple Sauce
3 lb. joint boned and rolled shoulder of pork

Apple sauce
1 lb. cooking apples
½ oz. PU margarine
2 oz. caster sugar
Rind and juice of half lemon
2 tbsps. water

1 Preheat rotisserie to maximum.
2 Impale joint on spit, and secure it centrally.
3 Fix spit in position and roast 30 min. per lb., i.e. 1½ hr. Lower heat if possible after 30 min.
4 Peel, core and slice apples.
5 Place in thick-based saucepan with PU margarine, water, lemon juice and rind. Cover and cook slowly until pulped.
6 Press through a sieve or beat well until smooth.
7 Add sugar. Serve hot.

If you are not the fortunate owner of a rotisserie, rest the joint on a wire rack over a deep roasting tin. Cook 55 min. per lb. i.e. 2¾ hr. at 350 or 4.

Spit roasting is recommended not only for its superb flavour, but because it is not standing bathed in its own fat. It is better for heart-watchers.

Escalopes of Veal
4 escalopes of veal
8 tomatoes
1 large onion
Clove of garlic
1 tbsp. PU oil
2 tbsps. chopped basil
1 oz. PU margarine
Salt and pepper

1 Peel and chop onion and garlic.
2 Place oil in saucepan, add onions and garlic and sauté gently.
3 Skin tomatoes and chop roughly. Add to pan.
4 Stir in chopped basil.
5 Season and leave to cook gently.

6 Melt PU margarine in frying pan and fry the escalopes slowly, basting frequently.
7 Remove cooked escalopes and keep hot on serving dish.
8 Turn the tomato sauce into the frying pan, to absorb meat juices. Heat thoroughly.
9 Pour sauce over veal and serve with boiled rice.

Veal is slightly higher in cholesterol than beef. This is because young muscles contain more cholesterol than middle-aged beef. This would counteract the fact that there is less fat in veal, and you should, therefore, not rush out and consume vast quantities in preference to other meats.

Roast Venison
1 haunch of venison, chine bone removed
4 oz. PU margarine
2 tbsps. plain flour

1 Light oven, 300 or 2.
2 Spread PU margarine all over joint. Wrap securely in aluminium foil.
3 Place in a roasting tin, foil folded on top.
4 Roast 25 min. per lb. Baste occasionally.
5 When nearly cooked, open out foil and dredge surface with flour. Baste. Leave foil open to allow joint to brown. An average haunch takes $2\frac{1}{2}$ to 3 hr.

Suitable sauces to serve with roast venison are red currant jelly, chestnut purée or cumberland sauce.

Venison should be hung 6 to 14 days before cooking to allow the flavour to develop and become 'high'. In season, June to December, venison is said to contain less cholesterol than any other meat.

9. Sauces, salad dressings, jams and preserves

Chocolate Custard Sauce

½ oz. cornflour
½ oz. cocoa
½ pint skimmed milk
1 oz. caster sugar
¼ tsp. rum (optional)

1 Blend cornflour with a little of the milk.
2 Heat remaining milk.
3 Pour hot milk onto paste. Stir in cocoa and sugar.
4 Return mixture to saucepan and bring to boil, stirring constantly.
5 Add rum and simmer 2 min.

Vanilla Custard Sauce

½ oz. cornflour
1 oz. caster sugar
½ pint skimmed milk
Vanilla essence

1 Blend cornflour with a little of the cold milk.
2 Add remainder of milk and stir well.
3 Place in saucepan over low heat. Stir constantly and bring to boil.
4 Add sugar and vanilla.
5 Stir and simmer 2 min.

Walnut Fudge

¼ pint skimmed milk
14 oz. caster sugar
2 oz. PU margarine
1 tsp. vanilla essence
1 oz. chopped walnuts

1 Place milk, PU margarine and sugar in a strong-based saucepan.
2 Heat gently until sugar is dissolved, then raise heat and bring to boil. Stir constantly.
3 Boil rapidly to 235°F or soft ball stage.
4 Toss in walnuts and add vanilla essence.
5 Leave to cool for 3 min. until a skin is visible on top.
6 Beat vigorously and as soon as mixture thickens, turn into greased square tin.
7 Mark into squares when cool, but do not cut until the fudge is cold.

Hazelnuts may be substituted for walnuts but are lower in PU acid value.

Glacé Icing

4 oz. icing sugar
3 tsps. warm water

1 Sieve icing sugar into mixing bowl.
2 Add water.
3 Beat until sugar has dissolved and is well blended. Consistency is correct when icing coats the back of a spoon.

Colour and flavour as desired.

Orange Icing: use orange juice in place of water with orange colouring.
Lemon Icing: use lemon juice in place of water with yellow colouring.
Strawberry Icing: use 3 tsps. strawberry juice or a few drops of strawberry flavouring and 3 tsps. water.
Coffee Icing: use 1 tsp. coffee essence and 2 tsps. water.

Orange Icing

3 oz. sieved icing sugar
1½ oz. PU margarine
Grated rind of 1 orange
1 tsp. orange juice

1 Cream the margarine until light and fluffy.
2 Gradually beat in icing sugar.
3 Add orange rind and juice.

Use as a filling or topping for cakes.

Lemon icing

3 oz. sieved icing sugar
1½ oz. PU margarine
Grated rind of 1 lemon
1 tsp. lemon juice

1 Cream the margarine until light and fluffy.
2 Gradually beat in icing sugar.
3 Add lemon rind and juice.

The sharpness of the lemon juice reduces the sweetness of this icing.

Stock Syrup

¼ pint water
8 oz. cube sugar

1 Place sugar and water in saucepan over low heat.
2 Stir until sugar is dissolved.
3 Bring to boil. Boil 1 min.

Stock syrup keeps well and when cool may be stored in refrigerator.

Apple Sauce

1 lb. cooking apples
½ oz. PU margarine
2 oz. caster sugar
Rind and juice of half lemon
2 tbsps. water

1 Peel, core and slice apples.
2 Place in thick based saucepan with PU margarine, water, lemon juice and rind.
3 Cover and cook slowly until pulped.
4 Press through a sieve or beat well until smooth.
5 Add sugar.
6 Reheat before serving.

Specifically served as an accompaniment to roast pork but very acceptable as a dessert.

In Holland apple sauce is very popular and is served with many different meals.

Apple sauce is often served to sufferers from diarrhoea because of its pectin content which helps create bulk in the intestinal contents.

Brandy Butter
2 oz. PU margarine
½ oz. ground almonds
1 oz. caster sugar
2 tsps. sweet sherry
2 tsps. brandy

1 Cream PU margarine and sugar until light and fluffy.
2 Add ground almonds.
3 Stir in sherry and brandy.
4 Serve cool.

Cranberry Sauce
6 oz. caster sugar
¼ pint water
8 oz. cranberries

1 Dissolve sugar in water in pan over low heat.
2 Add cranberries, stir and cook 12 to 15 min.
3 Crush fruit gently with potato masher.

Cumberland Sauce
3 tbsps. red currant jelly
1 tbsp. marmalade
½ wine glass port wine
Juice of ½ lemon
½ tsp. English mustard

1 Half melt jelly in a bowl over a pan of hot water.
2 Whisk in mustard, wine and lemon juice.
3 Stir in marmalade.
4 Leave to cool.

A sauce to enhance cold meats such as ham, chicken, game and venison.

White Sauce (using oil)
1 tbsp. PU oil
2 tbsps. flour
½ pint milk
¼ tsp. salt

1 Blend oil, flour, salt and a little milk in a saucepan.
2 Add remainder of milk and bring gently to boil stirring all the time. Continue to cook 1 to 2 min.

Add sweet or savoury ingredients as desired.
If using dried non-fat milk, use 2 heaped tbsps. powder and ½ pint cold water. Mix with other ingredients before heating.
Dried milk mixtures must always be heated slowly to achieve good results.

Béchamel Sauce
1 pint skimmed milk
1 small onion, quartered
1 piece of carrot
1 celery stalk, thickly sliced
1 clove of garlic
1 bay leaf
6 peppercorns
2 oz. PU margarine
2 oz. plain flour
Salt and pepper

1 Place milk in a saucepan. Add onion, carrot celery, garlic, bay leaf, peppercorns.
2 Heat gently until nearly boiling. Switch off heat.
3 Cover saucepan with lid and leave 15 min. to infuse.
4 Melt the margarine in another saucepan.

5 Stir in flour and blend to form a roux.
6 Strain infused milk gradually on to roux stirring constantly. Bring to boil to thicken. Cook 2 min.
7 Add seasoning to taste.

Béchamel is a superior white sauce for use with savoury dishes.

Brown Piquant Sauce

1 oz. PU margarine
1 oz. flour
½ pint water or stock
Salt and pepper
2 tsps. beef extract
1 small chopped carrot
1 small chopped onion
1 oz. mushrooms
Mace
1 Bay leaf
2 tsps. worcestershire sauce
2 or 3 tsps. tarragon vinegar
2 small gherkins
1 level tbsp. chopped capers

1 Melt margarine in pan, add flour, stir and fry gently until hazelnut brown.
2 Add liquid and other ingredients.
3 Add mushrooms whole.
4 Simmer 20 min. Strain into another saucepan.
5 Remove mushrooms, chop and return to sauce.

Caper Sauce

½ pint vegetable stock
1 oz. PU margarine
1 oz. flour
2 tbsps. roughly chopped capers
2 tsps. vinegar from capers
Salt and pepper

1 Using a teaspoon and small bowl, knead flour and PU margarine to form a paste.

2 Bring stock to boil, remove saucepan from heat and whisk in paste a little at a time.
3 When sauce is smooth, return saucepan to heat and bring to boil stirring constantly.
4 Stir in capers and vinegar and season to taste.

This coating sauce should be poured over *hot* fish or meat to achieve a smooth result.

Espagnole Sauce

1 oz. PU margarine
1 tsp. PU oil
1 lean rasher of bacon, chopped
½ onion, chopped
½ celery stalk, sliced
1 oz. mushrooms, sliced
1 small carrot, sliced
1 oz. plain flour
½ pint beef stock
1 level tbsp. tomato purée
1 bay leaf
1 or 2 sprigs parsley
Salt and pepper

1 Prepare vegetables.
2 Heat PU oil and PU margarine in saucepan.
3 Fry bacon until crisp.
4 Add onion, celery, carrot and mushrooms. Sauté 2 to 3 min.
5 Add flour. Stir and cook until fawn colour.
6 Stir in beef stock, then add parsley, bay leaf, tomato purée, salt and pepper. Simmer 25 min.
7 Remove bay leaf and liquidize or press through a sieve.

A classic brown sauce, espagnole is used extensively in hotels and restaurants, either by itself or as a foundation for other sauces. Used in meat dishes.

For lower cholesterol, the bacon may be omitted, and a soya protein bacon flavouring added at stage 6.

Parsley Sauce

1 oz. PU margarine
1 oz. plain flour
½ pint skimmed milk
2 tbsps. finely chopped parsley
Salt and pepper

1 Melt PU margarine in saucepan over low heat.
2 Stir in flour and cook ½ min.
3 Gradually add milk and bring to boil stirring all the time. Simmer 2 min.
4 Add parsley, salt and pepper.

Use more milk for a thinner sauce.

Anchovy Sauce

1 oz. PU margarine
1 oz. plain flour
½ pint skimmed milk
2 tsps. anchovy essence or 4 pounded anchovy fillets
Pepper

1 Melt PU margarine in saucepan over low heat.
2 Stir in flour and cook ½ min.
3 Gradually add milk and bring to boil stirring all the time. Simmer 2 min.
4 Add pepper and anchovy essence.

Fish stock may be substituted for skimmed milk.

Hot Tomato Sauce

½ pint canned tomato juice
½ oz. cornflour
Salt and pepper
Pinch sugar
Pinch nutmeg
Lemon juice to taste

1 Blend cornflour with a little of the juice.
2 Add remainder of juice and place in saucepan, heat, stirring constantly until thickened.
3 Add seasonings and lemon juice and simmer 5 min. on very low heat.

Very quick to prepare, this 'store cupboard' recipe is suitable for all dishes which require a coating sauce.

Bulgarian Salad Dressing

1 5-oz. carton low-fat yoghurt
1 tbsp. tarragon vinegar
1 tsp. English dry mustard powder
1 tsp. paprika
1 clove of garlic (crushed)
Pinch salt

1 Turn yoghurt into basin and whisk lightly.
2 Whisk in garlic, mustard, paprika, salt and vinegar.
3 Allow to stand 2 or 3 hr. before using.

French Dressing

$\frac{3}{4}$ pint (15 fl. oz.) PU oil
$\frac{1}{4}$ pint (5 fl. oz.) wine vinegar
$\frac{1}{4}$ tsp. salt
1 level tsp. french mustard
$\frac{1}{4}$ tsp. pepper

1 Combine salt, pepper mustard and vinegar in large jug.
2 Stir to dissolve salt.
3 Pour into large jar or wine bottle.
4 Add oil, place cork or lid on firmly and shake vigorously.

French dressing keeps indefinitely, but must be shaken before use each time it is required. The oil separates when left for a comparatively short time.

The proportion of oil to vinegar may be increased to 4:1 or reduced to 2:1 according to preference.

Non-cholesterol Mayonnaise

8 fl. oz. PU oil
2 level tbsps. soya flour
6 tbsps. water
3 tbsps. lemon juice
$\frac{1}{4}$ level tsp. dry mustard
$\frac{1}{2}$ level tsp. salt
Pinch white pepper
Pinch sugar

1 Beat together soya flour, mustard, salt, pepper, sugar and water.
2 Whisk oil into mixture drop by drop until mixture emulsifies and thickens.
3 Gently stir in lemon juice.
4 Use as required.

Variations of flavour can be produced by using tarragon or cider vinegar instead of lemon juice.

The mayonnaise will thicken and 'cook' if the bowl is placed over a pan of very hot water and whisked briskly.

No-oil Salad Dressing
1 small onion
4 or 5 sprigs of parsley
$\frac{1}{4}$ tsp. marjoram
$\frac{1}{4}$ tsp. white pepper
$\frac{1}{2}$ tsp. salt
$\frac{1}{2}$ tsp. sweet paprika
$\frac{1}{8}$ pt. (2 fl. oz.) wine vinegar
2 tsps. lemon juice
2 tbsps. water

1 Mince onion and parsley. Combine with other ingredients and chill 2 hr.

Stir before using.

If you have a liquidizer place all ingredients in goblet and run at medium speed for 1 min.

The dressing is sharp and aromatic, most suitable for those who prefer a 'vinegary' taste.

Apple and Blackberry Jam
2 lb. cooking apples
1$\frac{1}{2}$ lb. blackberries
$\frac{1}{2}$ pint water
3 lb. cube or preserving sugar
1 tbsp. PU oil

1 Peel, core and slice apples. Wash and drain blackberries.
2 Place in preserving pan with water. Bring to boil.
3 Cook until fruit is soft and mushy. Approx. 15 min.

4 Lower heat, add sugar and stir until dissolved.
5 When sugar crystals are all melted, raise heat and bring rapidly to boil. Do not stir at this stage.
6 Boil until jam reaches 220°F., or a little dropped on to a cold saucer wrinkles.
7 Switch off heat. Stir in PU oil.
8 Leave to cool a little, then pot and cover.

The yield is about 5 lb. To make a very quick yet superior jam, use 1½ lb. frozen apple slices and 1½ lb. frozen blackberries. Cube sugar is packed in 1 lb. cartons so that no weighing scales are necessary. Add 2 tbsps. of cheap brandy before stirring in the PU oil. This will give added flavour and help to preserve the jam.

Dried Fruit Preserve
4 oz. dried peaches
8 oz. dried apricots
4 oz. dried pears
1 Bramley apple, peeled and cored
Juice and rind of 1 lemon
3 lb. granulated sugar
3 pints water
3 oz. almonds, blanched and split
1 tbsp. PU oil

1 Soak dried fruit in cold water for 12 hr.
2 Drain and chop. Chop the apple.
3 Place chopped fruit in large saucepan or preserving pan with 3 pints of water.
4 Bring to boil and simmer until fruit is tender. Approx. 50 min.
5 Lower heat, add sugar, lemon juice, rind and almonds.
6 Stir until sugar is dissolved.
7 When sugar crystals have disappeared, raise heat and bring jam rapidly to boil. Continue boiling until setting point 220°F. is reached. Test by dropping a little of the syrup on to a cold plate when it should wrinkle as it cools.
8 Switch off heat and stir in PU oil.
9 Have five warmed jam jars ready to fill after the mixture has cooled for 5 min. Cover with waxed and cellophane discs and secure each jar with an elastic band.

Lemon and Rhubarb Conserve

3 lb. fresh rhubarb
2½ lb. caster sugar
Juice and rind of 3 lemons
2 level tsps. ground cinnamon
6 oz. raisins
4 oz. shelled walnuts

1 Chop the rhubarb and place in a thick-based saucepan or preserving pan with the sugar, lemon juice, rind and cinnamon.
2 Cook slowly stirring constantly until the mixture is soft and thick. Approx. 1 hr.
3 Remove scum.
4 Skin and chop the walnuts, chop the raisins and add both to the mixture.
5 Divide between four warmed 1 lb. jars.
6 Cover with waxed discs and cellophane jam pot covers.
7 Close with elastic bands.

Mincemeat

8 oz. currants
8 oz. raisins
8 oz. sultanas
4 oz. mixed chopped peel
2 oz. blanched almonds
1 lb. apples
2 lemons
2 tbsps. brandy
1 tsp. mixed spice
¼ tsp. salt
8 oz. PU margarine
12 oz. demerara sugar

1 Wash and dry currants, raisins and sultanas.
2 Mince currants, raisins, sultanas and almonds.
3 Grate rind of lemons and squeeze juice.
4 Peel, core and finely chop apples.
5 Blend minced mixture, lemon rind and juice, chopped apples in mixing bowl.
6 Add remaining ingredients and stir thoroughly.
7 Pack into clean jam jars.

Yield about four jars.

To keep in good condition pour a little melted PU margarine over mincemeat after potting, cover with self-sealing plastic film.

Walnut Orange Preserve

6 dessert oranges
2 oz. seedless raisins
2 oz. chopped mixed peel
2 lb. demerara sugar
2 oz. chopped walnuts
3 pints water

1 Wash oranges and grate rind.
2 Cut oranges into quarters lengthways, and remove peel, pith and pips.
3 Chop pulp coarsely.
4 Tie pips in small piece of muslin, and put in large saucepan with chopped orange, any juice remaining and water.
5 Bring to boil, and simmer until reduced to two thirds
6 Remove pips and discard.
7 Add rind, sugar and dried fruit, stir well and heat gently until sugar is dissolved.
8 Without stirring further, bring to boil, add walnuts and cook until setting point is reached.
9 Leave to cool a little, stir and fill warmed jam jars. Cover with waxed and cellophane discs and seal with elastic bands.

Test for setting point either using a thermometer which should register 220°F., or by dropping a tsp. of jam onto a cold saucer, when the jam should wrinkle.

Walnuts have the highest PU fat ratio of all the usual varieties of nut and contain 20 mg. of Vitamin E per 100 gm.

Tomato Chutney

12 oz. tomatoes
12 oz. firm apples
12 oz. seedless raisins
8 oz. demerara sugar
8 oz. shallots

¾ tsp. cayenne pepper
6 cloves
4 chillies (fresh or dried)
1 pint malt vinegar

1 Peel tomatoes and shallots. Peel and core apples.
2 Mince tomatoes, shallots, apples and raisins.
3 Place in saucepan over very low heat with sugar and cayenne pepper.
4 Add chillies and cloves tied in a small piece of muslin.
5 Cook 30 min. stirring frequently.
6 Add vinegar.
7 Simmer 3 hr.
8 Pour into warm dry jars. Cover and seal whilst hot.

Enough to fill five 1 lb. jars. Serve with meat or fish dishes.
Chutney is inclined to stick to the pan during cooking. Stirring is essential.
White vinegar gives a better appearance, but brown vinegar gives a better flavour.
The consistency should be fairly dry before adding vinegar. If mixture is too loose towards end of cooking, boil rapidly to reduce.

Yoghurt

1 pint skimmed milk reconstituted from non-fat granules
2 tsp. fresh low-fat commercial yoghurt

1 Bring milk *slowly* to boil.
2 Simmer 5 min.
3 Allow milk to cool to blood heat.
4 Whisk yoghurt into milk.
5 Cover and leave in warm place 5 to 6 hours.

If desired add chopped fresh fruit when yoghurt is set.

Pancake Batter

4 oz. plain flour
½ pint skimmed milk
2 egg whites
¼ tsp. salt
1 tbsp. PU oil
PU margarine for frying

1 Whisk milk into flour and salt.
2 Stir in PU oil.
3 Add beaten whites to batter and stir gently.
4 Set aside at least 30 min. and then use as required.

If you can purchase strong or bread flour, your pancakes will be near perfect. This flour has a higher gluten content which makes the batter more manageable. It is sometimes possible to buy gluten powder, a little of which may be added to plain or self-raising flour to strengthen it.

Apricot Custard Dessert

3 tbsps. apricot jam
4 egg whites
1 egg yolk
3 tsps. sugar
½ tsp. vanilla essence
¾ pint skimmed milk
2 oz. grated walnuts

1 Spread jam over base of soufflé dish.
2 Beat eggs lightly with sugar and vanilla.
3 Warm milk, but do not boil and pour onto egg mixture
4 Blend and strain through sieve into soufflé dish.
5 Stand in a tin half full of hot water.
6 Cover with a circle of greaseproof paper, greased on the underside.
7 Bake 350 or 4, 1 hr. or until firm to touch.
8 Leave to cool and then top with grated walnuts.

A good choice for a cold sweet. Apricot custard dessert will keep in the refrigerator for a few days. The walnuts provide a useful quantity of linoleic acid so necessary in the low cholesterol diet.

Although there is an egg yolk in this recipe, it will only work out at ¼ egg per person which equals 107 mg. cholesterol.

Banana Brulée

4 bananas
2 5-oz. cartons low-fat yoghurt
4 level tbsps. demerara sugar

1 Peel and slice bananas and half fill four individual oven-proof soufflé dishes.
2 Cover with yoghurt ($\frac{1}{2}$ carton each) and smooth with palette knife. Chill for one hr.
3 Cover with sugar and pat down with palette knife.
4 Preheat grill.
5 Place dishes under grill until sugar has dissolved and caramelized.
6 Leave to cool before serving.

To obtain a really crisp brittle topping, the dishes must be as near the grill element as possible.

Only direct-heatproof dishes are suitable to use.

Incredibly quick to prepare, Banana Brulée is suitable for special guests as well as a regular family sweet.

Bitter Sweet Stuffed Peaches

1 large can peach halves
2 oz. ground almonds
1 oz. caster sugar
1 oz. icing sugar
1 egg white
$\frac{1}{4}$ pint water
8 oz. granulated sugar

1 Drain peaches and rinse under cold water.
2 Put ground almonds, caster sugar and icing sugar in bowl and add sufficient egg white to bind.
3 Place a heaped tsp. of mixture in hollows of half of the peach halves and place in ovenproof glass or stainless steel serving dish.
4 Place remaining peach halves on top to resemble whole peaches.
5 Place water and granulated sugar in saucepan and dissolve over low heat.
6 Bring to boil and cook rapidly until syrup is dark brown but not burnt.

7 Immediately pour syrup over peaches to coat.
8 Leave to cool and then place in refrigerator for at least 12 hr.

Serve cold.
When first poured on to the peaches the syrup forms a brittle toffee like crust. This later dissolves to a bitter sweet sauce.
To clean saucepan: fill with hot water and leave until remaining toffee dissolves.

Bread and 'Butter' Pudding
6 to 8 large slices of bread
1½ oz. PU margarine
1½ oz. currants
1½ oz. raisins
2 oz. caster sugar
1 pint skimmed milk
2 egg whites
½ tsp. vanilla essence
Grated nutmeg
2 level tbsps. demerara sugar

1 Remove crusts from bread and spread with PU margarine.
2 Cut each slice into four triangles.
3 Arrange layers of bread (margarine side up), dried fruit and caster sugar in deep greased pie dish. The top layer should be bread.
4 Warm the milk and stir into lightly beaten egg whites. Add vanilla essence.
5 Strain over bread mixture.
6 Sprinkle top with grated nutmeg and demerara sugar.
7 Bake 325 or 3. Approx. 1½ hr. until brown.

Caramelized Oranges
2 large oranges
6 oz. caster sugar
¼ pt. water

1 Place water and sugar in pan over low heat until dissolved.
2 Remove thin layer of peel from one orange and cut into 'julienne' strips.

3 Peel oranges and slice horizontally.
4 Reassemble oranges and place on ovenproof serving dish.
5 Place strips of peel in boiling water and cook 1 min. Strain.
6 Bring syrup to boil until brown. DO NOT STIR.
7 Add 2 tsps. boiling water and julienne strips.
8 Pour immediately over oranges.

Serve cold, garnished with fresh mint.
A refreshing dessert to follow a more solid main course.

Cherry Pavlova
Whites of 3 standard eggs
1 level tsp. cornflour
1 tsp. white vinegar
1 tsp. water
7 oz. caster sugar

1 Light oven, 300 or 2.
2 Place egg whites in clean bowl and whisk until stiff.
3 Blend cornflour, vinegar and water. Add to mixture.
4 Add sugar and whisk until mixture is heavy and smooth.
5 Place sheet of vegetable parchment on baking tray and spoon on to centre.
6 Shape into round 1 in. thick.
7 Lower heat to 275 or 1, and place pavlova on centre shelf.
8 After 1 hr., switch off current and leave to cool without opening oven.

When cool decorate with

Topping
1 oz. sugar
1 oz. flour
¼ pint skimmed milk
Vanilla essence
¼ oz. PU margarine
5 oz. carton low-fat yoghurt
1 Small can drained red cherries

1 Blend sugar with flour and a little of the milk.
2 Stir in remainder of milk and vanilla essence, and bring to boil to thicken.

3 Beat in margarine and carton of yoghurt.
4 Leave to cool and then spread over centre of pavlova and decorate with cherries.

Be sure to buy low-fat or non-fat yoghurt or yoghurt made from skimmed milk.

If the topping is too thick, thin down with cherry juice but take care, the pavlova is very sweet in itself and a sharper topping makes a good contrast.

Cherry Snow
1 lb. juicy black or white cherries
¼ pint water
2 level tbsps. granulated sugar
2 egg whites
1 tsp. cherry brandy

1 Wash fruit, remove stalks and poach gently in water until soft.
2 Stir in sugar until dissolved.
3 Press fruit through a sieve to extract pulp and remove stones.
4 Cool purée, and refrigerate until quite cold. Stir in cherry brandy.
5 Beat egg whites until stiff but not dry.
6 Stir one tbsp. of egg white into purée. Fold in remaining egg white.
7 Serve chilled.

A cherry-stoner is a useful gadget for cherries or cherry plums. If you have one, remove the stones which are to be discarded before cooking.

Chocolate Pyramids
3 oz. PU margarine
3 oz. castor sugar
4 oz. plain flour
1 level tbsp. cocoa
1 level tsp. baking powder
Pinch salt

1 oz. chopped walnuts
2 oz. chopped peel
4 oz. chopped dates
1 to 2 tbsps. skimmed milk

1 Cream PU margarine and sugar until light and fluffy.
2 Sieve in flour, cocoa, baking powder and salt.
3 Add nuts, peel and dates. Mix well.
4 Add milk. Mixture should be fairly stiff.
5 Place spoonsful of mixture on greased baking sheet.
6 Pinch tops with fingertips to form pyramid shapes.
7 Bake 375 or 5, 20 min.

Chocolate Rice Dessert

2 oz. ground rice
1 tbsp. sieved cocoa
1 pint skimmed milk
1 oz. demerara sugar
½ tsp. rum
Few drops vanilla essence
1 tbsp. chopped walnut
1 heaped tbsp. apricot jam

1 Blend rice, cocoa and sugar with a little cold milk.
2 Heat remainder of milk until hot but not boiling.
3 Pour hot milk over rice mixture, stir and return to saucepan.
4 Stir until boiling. Lower heat and simmer 5 min. stirring continuously.
5 Remove from heat. Add rum and vanilla.
6 Spread jam over base of serving dish.
7 Cover with rice mixture and leave until cold.
8 Sprinkle with chopped walnuts.

Christmas Pudding

4 oz. raisins
4 oz. currants
4 oz. sultanas
4 oz. mixed peel
4 oz. soft dark brown sugar
4 oz. breadcrumbs
2 oz. plain flour

1 level tbsp. soya flour
1 level tsp. salt
1 small grated carrot
2 oz. chopped walnuts or almonds
4 oz. PU margarine
½ level tsp. mixed spice
Grated rind and juice of 1 lemon
Grated rind and juice of 1 sweet orange
1 small grated apple
2 tbsps. brandy
4 egg whites

1 Clean dried fruit.
2 Mix all ingredients together. Cover and stand 24 hr.
3 If mixture is too stiff, add a little skimmed milk to loosen to dropping consistency.
4 Place in one large or two small greased basins.
5 Cover with greased greaseproof paper and tie with muslin or cover with pleated foil.
6 Steam 5 or 6 hr.
7 Leave to cool. Remove coverings and replace with clean greased greaseproof and muslin.
8 Leave until required and then steam 2 hr. before serving.

Serve with custard (see page 111), or brandy butter (see page 114).

Crème Brulée
½ pint skimmed milk
3 egg whites
1 tsp. soya flour
½ tsp. vanilla essence
½ oz. caster sugar
Extra caster sugar for topping

1 Blend soya flour with milk and heat but do not boil.
2 Beat egg whites until frothy.
3 Stir milk into egg whites. Add sugar and vanilla essence.
4 Strain into three or four individual soufflé dishes.
5 Place moulds in baking tin half filled with warm water.
6 Bake on middle shelf 350 or 4, 30 to 40 min. until just set in centre. Leave to cool.
7 Chill 2 hr.

8 Preheat grill. Sprinkle surface of pudding with caster sugar. Place under fierce heat for 1 min. to caramelize.
9 Leave to cool and set.

Hitherto this dessert was forbidden to 'dieters' because of the high proportion of egg yolks. This modified recipe is quite safe and most acceptable.

Crêpes Suzettes
½ pint pancake batter
PU oil
4 oz. PU margarine
1 oz. caster sugar
Grated rind and juice of one orange
4 tbsps. cointreau, curaçao or grand marnier
2 tbsps. brandy

1 Pour a little batter into a heated oiled omelette or small frying pan. Tip handle of pan to spread mixture. When centre is opaque, turn pancake and cook for a few seconds.
2 Stack pancakes between sheets of greaseproof paper. Make 12 pancakes. Keep warm in oven on low heat.
3 Melt PU margarine in frying pan.
4 Add sugar, orange rind and juice and liqueur and bring to boil.
5 Fold pancakes in four. Place in frying pan two at a time to coat with syrup.
6 Remove to hot serving dish.
7 Bring syrup to boil, add brandy and flambé (set alight).
8 Pour over pancakes. Serve at once.

The first pancake often sticks and is a little too thick. Do not serve this one to your guests.

French Apple Tart
4 oz. plain flour
3 oz. PU margarine
Pinch salt
Cold water

1 oz. PU margarine
2 oz. castor sugar
2 lb. cooking apples

1 Make pastry. Rub 1½ oz. PU margarine into flour and salt.
2 Add sufficient cold water to form a paste.
3 Wrap in polythene bag and place in refrigerator 30 min.
4 Roll pastry into oblong.
5 Place dabs of remaining 1½ oz. of PU margarine over two thirds of pastry.
6 Fold uncovered one third pastry over middle one third and cover with remaining one third pastry.
7 Turn so that open ends are facing you and fold is at side.
8 Roll pastry into oblong and fold into three.
9 Repeat rolling and then roll into shape ½ in. bigger than your ovenproof baking dish. Leave in refrigerator while preparing filling.
10 Melt margarine in pan and stir in sugar. Continue stirring over low heat until mixture turns light brown. Remove from heat.
11 Peel, quarter and core apples.
12 Lay apple quarters in base of pie dish.
13 Pour sauce over apples.
14 Damp edges of pastry. Cover pie dish with the pastry and seal well. Knock up edges.
15 Bake in oven, 400 or 6; 30 to 40 min.
16 Run knife around edge of pastry to loosen, and then turn upside down on to a hot serving dish.

Do not use frozen apple slices, they may overcook and become mushy.

Fresh Fruit Salad
A selection of fresh fruit in season
Lemon juice
Stock syrup (page 113)

1 Wash and dry fruit.
2 Prepare in usual way and cut into even sized pieces. Apples and peaches need not be peeled.
3 Sprinkle fruit with lemon juice and arrange in serving bowl.
4 Pour a little stock syrup over fruit to moisten and coat.

Apples, pears and bananas should be prepared last as they discolour when in contact with the air.

Colour and texture are important. The following combinations are suggested:

(a) Apple, banana, orange, grapes.
(b) Pear, pineapple, cherries, banana.
(c) Banana, cherries, apricot, apple.
(d) Orange, strawberries, apple, grapes.
(e) Peach, strawberries, apple, banana.
(f) Apricots, pear, strawberries, orange.
(g) Pineapple, peach, cherries, apple.

Allow 4 oz. of fruit per person before preparation.

Ginger, Peel and Treacle Roly-Poly Pudding

6 oz. plain flour
2 level tsps. baking powder
½ level tsp. salt
3 oz. PU margarine
6 tbsps. cold water
2 heaped tbsps. black treacle
1 heaped tbsp. chopped mixed peel
1 piece preserved ginger (the size of a walnut)

1 Half fill large saucepan with boiling water.
2 Sieve flour, salt and baking powder into mixing bowl.
3 Rub in PU margarine to breadcrumb stage.
4 Add water to mix to soft dough.
5 Knead dough gently and flatten into an oblong ¼ in. thick.
6 Spread treacle over dough leaving ¾ in. border on one short side and two long sides.
7 Sprinkle chopped peel and sliced ginger over treacle.
8 Damp edges of pastry and roll up from covered short end to form a swiss roll shape. Seal ends.
9 Grease a double sheet of foil and wrap roly-poly securely in it.
10 Lower into saucepan, reduce heat to simmer and cover with lid. Cook 2 to 2½ hr.

Continental cookery being so popular now, it makes a refreshing change to serve this 'Olde English' type pudding. The PU margarine in replacing the traditional suet reduces the stodginess.

Ginger Soufflé

1 oz. PU margarine
1 tsp. soya flour
1 oz. plain flour
1 oz. caster sugar
Scant ¼ pint skimmed milk
1 egg yolk
5 egg whites
1 tbsp. ginger syrup
2 or 3 pieces of stem ginger finely chopped

1 Melt PU margarine in saucepan.
2 Add flour and soya flour. Stir over low heat.
3 Gradually add milk and ginger syrup. Stir until mixture forms a ball that leaves sides of pan.
4 Remove from heat. Leave to cool a little.
5 Stir in egg yolk. Add chopped ginger.
6 Beat egg whites until stiff but not dry.
7 Fold sugar into egg whites.
8 Fold egg whites gently into cooked mixture.
9 Turn into greased 7 in. soufflé dish.
10 Bake 375 or 5; 25 min. until firm in centre.
11 Serve immediately.

Stem ginger in syrup is easily obtainable and keeps indefinitely.

Junket

½ pint skimmed milk
½ oz. caster sugar
½ tsp. essence of rennet
¼ tsp. vanilla essence
Grated nutmeg

1 Heat milk to blood heat.
2 Stir in sugar.
3 Add vanilla essence.
4 Remove from heat and add rennet.
5 Divide into individual glasses. The mixture is liquid at this stage.

6 Leave in a warm place for 15 to 20 min. to give the enzymes time to work.

7 When set, sprinkle with nutmeg and chill before serving.

Rennet clots at blood heat. It is used to thicken milk mixtures in invalid cookery.

Lemon Meringue Pie

4 oz. plain flour
2 oz. PU margarine
1 level tbsp. icing sugar
Cold skimmed milk (approx. 2 tbsps.)

2 level tbsps. cornflour
¼ pint water
½ oz. PU margarine
Grated rind and juice of 1 lemon
1 oz. caster sugar

2 egg whites
4 oz. caster sugar

1 Sieve flour and icing sugar into mixing bowl.
2 Rub in 2 oz. PU margarine until mixture resembles breadcrumbs.
3 Add sufficient cold skimmed milk to form a dough. Use a knife to mix.
4 Roll out paste and line a 6 in. flan ring.
5 Refrigerate or freeze 30 min.
6 Bake blind 400 or 6, 15 min., remove foil and continue baking 5 min. more. Remove from oven, take off flan ring.
7 Lower oven temperature to 300 or 2.
8 Prepare filling. Place cornflour, water, margarine, lemon juice, lemon rind and 1 oz. caster sugar in a saucepan.
9 Whisk continuously over moderate heat.
10 Bring to boil and cook 2 min. until thickened.
11 Pour mixture into pastry case.
12 Whisk egg whites until stiff, add half (2 oz.) caster sugar and whisk until stiff once more.
13 Fold in remaining (2 oz.) caster sugar with metal spoon.
14 Pile over lemon filling, covering to edges completely.

15 To make peaks, lift mixture with point of knife.
16 Place flan on baking tray and brown in middle of oven 20 to 30 min.

Lemon Pancakes

½ pint pancake batter
1 tbsp. caster sugar
1 lemon
PU margarine for frying

1 Prepare pancake batter (see page 124)
2 Place knob of PU margarine in 8 in. frying pan and heat.
3 When very hot, pour in small quantity of batter and swirl round pan until the base is completely covered with the mixture.
4 Lower heat.
5 When mixture is opaque and set, turn or toss pancake.
6 Cook for a few moments, then turn on to hot plate.
7 Sprinkle with sugar, roll up with fork and squeeze lemon juice on top, or slice lemon and make butterflies to garnish.

The recipe makes about 8 pancakes.

Before making pancakes, 'prove' the frying pan. Place a knob of PU margarine in pan with a tsp. of salt. Heat pan and when margarine has melted and starts to turn brown, remove from heat and carefully wipe out with kitchen paper. This process leaves the pan with a smooth greased base.

Orange Jelly Shells

3 large oranges
½ oz. (1 packet) gelatine
1 level tbsp. granulated sugar
Hot water

1 Dissolve gelatine in ¼ pint hot water.
2 Add sugar.
3 Squeeze oranges, reserving shells, and add juice to gelatine mixture.
4 Make liquid up to 1 pint with hot water.
5 Rest orange shells in dessert dishes and divide jelly between them.
6 Leave to set.

Setting can be hastened if cooled jellies are placed in refrigerator.

Decorate with a sprig of fresh mint.

Orange Snow Caps

1 large orange
1 small eating apple
4 glacé cherries
1 oz. ground almonds or grated walnuts
Broken digestive biscuits or crumbs
1 eggwhite
3 oz. icing sugar

1 Light oven, 400 or 6.
2 Cut orange in half and scoop out all pulp with grapefruit knife.
3 Chop orange pulp roughly using knife and fork, on a plate, remove excess pith and pips. Squeeze oranges with hands to remove surplus juice.
4 Peel and core apple and chop. Mix with orange pulp and juice.
5 Chop cherries and add to mixture.
6 Add nuts and sufficient crumbled biscuits to absorb juices.
7 Divide mixture between orange shells. The mixture should reach the top edges of the oranges.
8 Prepare a meringue with egg white and icing sugar, whisking over hot water to stiffen.
9 Place meringue in forcing bag with star nozzle and pipe pyramids to cover orange filling.
10 Gently place oranges in ovenproof dish and brown in oven for just 5 min.
11 Remove oranges carefully from dish and leave to cool.
12 Serve cold.

Do not overbake oranges as they will become bitter. The meringue will soften after cooking, and should be soft and mallowy inside. Orange Snow Caps will keep 2 or 3 days in refrigerator.

Peach Condé

2 oz. round rice
1 pint skimmed milk
1 oz. caster sugar
Few drops vanilla essence
1 small can sliced peaches
Orange colouring
1 level tsp. arrowroot

1 Wash rice and place in greased saucepan with milk.
2 Stir over low heat until boiling.
3 Lower heat, cover and simmer gently until rice has absorbed milk and is cooked, 20 min.
4 Remove from heat, stir in sugar and vanilla.
5 Rinse four dariole moulds with cold water.
6 Divide rice between moulds and press well down.
7 Place in a cool place until quite cold.
8 Turn out onto serving dish.
9 Decorate with peach slices.
10 Pour peach syrup into small saucepan.
11 Stir in 1 tsp. arrowroot and cook over low heat until syrup boils and thickens. Cook 1 min. stirring continuously.
12 Add colouring.
13 Pour syrup over puddings.

Dariole moulds are often used for baking 'madeleines', light individual sponge cakes traditionally coated with desiccated coconut and decorated with glacé cherries. These are not suitable in a low cholesterol diet, but an adapted recipe is on page 161.

Raspberry Whip

1 lb. raspberries (fresh or frozen)
1 egg white
2½ oz. icing sugar

1 Pulp raspberries with fork or wooden spoon.
2 Place egg white and sugar in bowl resting on pan of hot water and whisk until very thick. About 15 min.

3 Fold raspberries into meringue mixture.
4 Serve chilled in individual dishes.

If you have a table model electric mixer there will be no need to whisk over hot water. It will take about 5 min.

Sherried Plums

1 lb. under-ripe Victoria plums
2 level tbsps. soft brown sugar
2 level tbsps. sweet sherry

1 Wash plums and leave whole.
2 Lay plums in thick-bottomed saucepan.
3 Sprinkle sugar over plums and put well-fitting lid on saucepan.
4 Place pan on lowest possible heat, cook, shaking pan occasionally until skins split.
5 Add sherry. Replace lid and continue cooking until plums are tender, resting in a thick dark rich syrup.

Cooking can take from 30 min. to 1 hr. depending on the heat, but the lower the heat the better the flavour.

If your lid is not tight-fitting enough, lay a sheet of foil 1 in. wider than the diameter of saucepan over the pan and then put lid on top of the foil.

Strawberry Cornflour Mould

2½ oz. cornflour
1 pint skimmed milk
1 oz. sugar
8 oz. frozen strawberries
Colouring

1 Reserve a few strawberries for decoration. Turn remainder into dish and sprinkle with sugar. Leave to thaw.
2 Blend cornflour with a little of the cold milk.
3 Heat remainder of milk in saucepan and pour onto cornflour mixture. Stir.
4 Return to saucepan and bring to boil, stirring constantly. Simmer 2 min.
5 Press thawed strawberries through a mouli-lègumes or sieve.

6 Stir into thickened mixture. Colour red if required.
7 Rinse mould in cold water and pour in mixture.
8 Turn out when cold and decorate with remaining strawberries.

Cornflour is pure starch and the grains will burst and
gelatinize at 212°F.

Starch mixtures will not thicken unless brought to the
boil.

Syrup Pyramid
4 oz. plain flour
½ oz. sugar
Pinch of salt
1½ level tsps. baking powder
½ oz. PU margarine
2 fl. oz. skimmed milk
1 egg white
½ lb. warmed golden syrup
Chopped pistachio nuts
PU oil for deep fat frying
Draining paper

1 Sieve flour, salt, baking powder and sugar into mixing
  bowl.
2 Rub in PU margarine.
3 Stir milk into egg white and then add to dry ingredients.
4 Mix to a smooth dough.
5 Cover with a damp cloth and leave to rest 20 min.
6 Heat PU oil in deep saucepan.
7 Knead the dough gently with floured hands, divide into
  pieces and roll each to the size of a marble.
8 Fry until golden brown, placing balls in the oil one at a
  time to prevent them sticking together.

Syrup pyramid

9 Drain quickly and drop into warmed golden syrup to coat.
10 When all balls are ready, form into a pyramid on a hot serving dish and sprinkle with chopped pistachio nuts.

This unusual sweet is made the more interesting if served with stewed dried fruits. These can be placed in the centre of the dish inside the pyramid.

It is always best to use a thermometer when deep fat frying, for fat that is not hot enough will seep into the food, and if it is too hot, it will burn and become rancid. Oil has a smoking point of 400°F. and generally speaking frying should take place at a temperature between 360 and 375°F. If no thermometer is available test the oil by dropping a cube of bread into it. Count 20 and if the bread is golden brown the temperature is suitable.

Syrup Sponge Pudding
4 oz. self-raising flour
2 oz. caster sugar
3 tbsps. PU oil
2 egg whites
Skimmed milk
2 tbsps. golden syrup

1 Grease 1 lb. pudding basin with PU margarine.
2 Spoon golden syrup into basin.
3 Sieve flour and sugar into mixing bowl.
4 Stir unbeaten egg whites into oil with 1 tbsp. skimmed milk.
5 Stir liquid into dry mixture to form a very soft dough. Add more milk if necessary.
6 Turn onto syrup in prepared basin. Cover with greased foil.
7 Steam 1 hr.

The foil should be pleated to allow for expansion.
This size pudding will take 20 min. if cooked in a pressure cooker.

Toffee Banana Fritters

4 level tbsps. plain flour
5 tbsps. water
2 tbsps. red wine
Pinch salt
1 egg white
4 large under-ripe bananas
Lemon juice
PU oil
1 tbsp. sesame seeds (optional)

Syrup
8 oz. granulated sugar
¼ pint water
Few drops rose water
Pinch of cream of tartar

1 Mix flour with water and wine to a smooth batter.
2 Beat egg white until stiff but not dry.
3 Blend egg and salt with batter. Add sesame seeds.
4 Peel bananas, cut into 1 in. chunks, sprinkle with lemon juice and drop into batter.
5 One third fill pan with PU oil and bring to 360°F.
6 Lift out pieces of banana as required, using a perforated spoon, and fry in small quantities until golden brown.
7 Drain and keep hot.

Syrup
8 Dissolve the sugar slowly in water and rose water. Add pinch of cream of tartar.
9 Bring to boil and continue boiling until bubbles become large and gradually turn golden, 238°F.
10 Dip base of pan carefully in cold water to stop burning.
11 Gently drop the fritters into the syrup, and when they are coated remove them and immerse in a bowl of cold water.
12 Drain and serve.

Should you need to leave the bananas for a short time before cooking them, a sprinkle of lemon juice will prevent discoloration.

Vacherin

4 egg whites

8 oz. caster sugar

2 lb. raspberries, strawberries or blackberries or a mixture of all three

1 level tbsp. cornflour

½ tsp. vanilla essence

1 tbsp. granulated sugar

½ pint skimmed milk

1 tsp. PU margarine

1 sheet vegetable parchment or foil

1 Light oven, 275 or 1.

2 Line baking sheet with vegetable parchment.

3 Whisk the egg whites until stiff.

4 Add one third caster sugar and whisk again until very stiff.

5 Fold in remaining caster sugar with metal spoon.

6 Put mixture in forcing bag fitted with ½ in. plain nozzle.

7 Pipe a round base about 6 in. diameter on lined baking tray. Pipe mixture around edges building up layer by layer until a meringue 'wall' is formed.

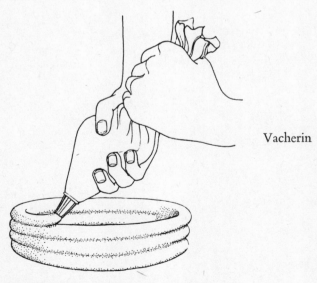

Vacherin

8 Bake until dry and just coloured.

9 Leave to cool.
10 Blend cornflour with a little of the cold milk.
11 Heat remainder of milk with the granulated sugar and vanilla essence.
12 Pour mixture hot but not boiling onto slaked cornflour. Blend and return to saucepan.
13 Bring to boil to thicken, whisking all the time.
14 Remove from heat and stir in PU margarine.
15 Cover with wet greaseproof paper, wet side against custard. Leave to cool.
16 Fill vacherin with layers of custard, fruit and sugar finishing with fruit.

Take care when adding vanilla essence. Some are stronger than others. It is therefore wise to measure in a spoon or lid of bottle before adding to mixture.

11. Bread, cakes and biscuits

Black Treacle Sticky Bread

1 oz. fresh yeast
¼ pint warm water
1 lb. plain flour
1 level tsp. salt
6 tbsps. black treacle
1 oz. PU margarine

1 Warm the water to blood heat. Add the yeast and stir until dissolved.
2 Sieve flour and salt into warmed mixing bowl.
3 Melt treacle and PU margarine over gentle heat. Do not allow mixture to become hot.
4 Add yeast and treacle mixture to flour. Mix to a soft sticky dough.
5 Cover with a damp cloth and leave in a warm place until doubled in bulk. Approx. 1½ hr.
6 Knead gently. Turn into greased 2 lb. loaf tin. Leave to prove 15 min.
7 Bake 400 or 6; 35 min. Leave to cool a little before turning out.

Date and Walnut Tea Bread

6 oz. self-raising flour
Pinch salt
½ level tsp. bicarbonate of soda
1 level tsp. cream of tartar
2 oz. chopped dates

1 oz. chopped walnuts
¼ pint buttermilk (made from skimmed milk)
1 level tbsp. treacle
1 oz. PU margarine

1 Preheat oven, 350 or 4.
2 Grease and line 1 lb. loaf tin.
3 Sift together flour, bicarbonate of soda, cream of tartar and salt.
4 Add chopped dates and walnuts.
5 Warm buttermilk, treacle, and PU margarine gently.
6 Add to dry ingredients and mix quickly.
7 Cover lightly with a piece of greased foil. Bake 30 to 40 min.

Wrap tightly in foil and keep 24 hr. before cutting. This will enable the fruity flavour to develop.

When purchasing buttermilk read the list of ingredients, since some manufacturers add cream and this of course is unsuitable.

Malt Loaf
½ oz. fresh yeast
⅛ pint warm water
½ lb. plain flour
½ level tsp. salt
2 level tbsps. malt extract
1 level tbsp. black treacle
½ oz. PU margarine

Glaze
1 heaped tbsp. sugar
2 tbsps. water

1 Dissolve yeast in the water.
2 Place malt, treacle and PU margarine in saucepan and melt over gentle heat.
3 Mix flour and salt in dry warmed bowl.
4 Pour yeast and malt mixtures over flour and beat well to a soft dough.
5 Turn onto floured board and knead thoroughly.
6 Flatten into oblong shape and then roll up, swiss roll fashion.

7 Press lightly into a well greased 1 lb. loaf tin.
8 Cover with a damp cloth or greased polythene bag and leave to rise in a warm place until mixture is doubled in size (about 1½ hr.).
9 Preheat oven, 400 or 6, and bake middle shelf 30 to 40 min.
10 Place sugar and water in saucepan and stir over low heat When dissolved, raise heat and stop stirring. Bring to boiling point and allow to boil 1 min.
11 When bread is ready, place on wire tray and spoon syrup over top and sides.

If using dried yeast, the method is slightly different: ¼ oz. dried yeast is the equivalent of ½ oz. fresh yeast. The yeast should be whisked lightly into the water with 1 tsp. sugar. Allow to stand 10 to 15 min. before adding to flour.

Malt extract is obtainable from chemists and health food stores. Golden syrup may replace black treacle but the bread will be a lighter colour.

Farmhouse Scones
8 oz. plain flour
2 oz. PU margarine
1 oz. caster sugar
Pinch salt
1 level tsp. bicarbonate of soda
2 level tsps. cream of tartar
1 oz. sultanas
Approx. ¼ pint skimmed milk

1 Sieve flour, salt, bicarbonate of soda and cream of tartar into mixing bowl.
2 Rub in PU margarine.
3 Add sugar.
4 Mix in enough milk to form soft dough.
5 Add sultanas, turn onto floured board and knead gently.
6 Roll dough to ¾ in. thick.
7 Cut out rounds with 2 in. cutter or cut into triangular wedges with sharp knife.
8 Brush tops with skimmed milk.
9 Place scones on greased baking tray.
10 Bake in preheated oven, 425 or 7; 10 to 15 min.

Soft Dinner Rolls

1 lb. plain flour
2 level tsps. salt
1 oz. fresh yeast or $\frac{1}{2}$ oz. dried yeast
4 tbsps. warm water
$\frac{1}{2}$ pint warm skimmed milk
2 oz. PU margarine

1 Sieve flour and salt into mixing bowl.
2 Blend yeast with warm water.
3 Melt PU margarine in the milk.
4 Add dissolved yeast, warm milk and PU margarine to flour and knead in bowl for 10 min. The dough should be fairly soft.
5 Cover with damp cloth or plastic film and leave in a warm place to rise.
6 When double in size and spongy, turn on to a floured board and knead gently.
7 Divide into 16 or 20 pieces.
8 Knead each piece gently to smooth the mixture and shape into an oval. Pinch the ends slightly.
9 Place on greased baking sheets making sure the rolls do not touch.
10 Light oven, 450 or 8. Place small dish of hot water on base of oven.
11 When oven has reached the correct temperature, put the rolls in to bake.
12 Lower heat to 400 or 6 after 5 min. Continue baking for a further 10 to 15 min.

Brush the rolls with skimmed milk or water and sprinkle with poppy seeds before baking if desired.

Do not overheat the liquid as this will kill the yeast.

The small dish of hot water in the oven helps to keep the bread mixture soft.

Croûtons

2 or 3 slices day-old bread
4 or more tbsps. PU oil

1. Cut bread into slices $\frac{1}{2}$ in thick.
2. Remove crusts.

3 Cut each slice into 'fingers' ½ in. wide.
4 Cut across 'fingers' at ½ in. intervals. You should now have even-sized cubes.
5 Put PU oil into frying pan. Switch on heat and shallow-fry croutons in hot oil, a few at a time, until golden. Toss with a fish slice so that all sides are crispened.
6 Drain on absorbent paper.
7 Serve hot.

Drop a few sizzling croûtons into hot soup at moment of serving.

Croûtons absorb much oil so use more than you think is needed. If the bread absorbs all the oil in the pan and the croûtons are not cooked, add more oil, a little at a time, so that the temperature is not drastically reduced.

Sprinkle fried croûtons with paprika for a more pungent flavour.

Croûtes are rounds of bread ¼ in. thick fried as above.

Store croûtons or croûtes in a plastic container with well-fitting lid. Keep in the refrigerator for a few days or 1 month in the freezer. Reheat in a hot oven.

Fried Breadcrumbs
4 oz. fresh white breadcrumbs
3 tbsps. PU oil

1 Toss breadcrumbs in hot PU oil until golden brown.
2 Drain on absorbent paper. Use as desired.

Add a sprinkling of fried breadcrumbs to savoury dishes when the diet is deficient in PU acids.

To make fresh breadcrumbs, rub on a grater or use an electric liquidizer. A parsmint is a small gadget for chopping parsley, and may be used for making small quantities of breadcrumbs.

Melba Toast
Slices of medium thick cut bread.

1 Toast slices of bread lightly on both sides.
2 Remove crusts.
3 While still hot, lay toast on chopping board.

4 Rest palm of hand on toast and split each slice nearly through (horizontally along *length* of slice) using a sharp knife.

5 Without withdrawing knife, hold toast vertically on board and press blade of knife down to separate halves.

6 Cut resulting slices in half diagonally and toast the cut sides until the corners curl up.

Use within a few hours, or store in an airtight tin and crispen in a hot oven before serving.

Chelsea Buns

Dough
8 oz. plain or strong flour
1 to 2 oz. caster sugar
Pinch salt
1½ oz. PU margarine
½ beaten egg
½ oz. yeast
¼ pint warm skimmed milk

Filling
Melted PU margarine (approx. 1½ oz.)
2 oz. currants
1 level tsp. mixed spice

Bun Wash
2 oz. caster sugar
4 tbsps. water.

1 Sieve flour and salt into warmed mixing bowl, and add sugar.

2 Rub in 1½ oz. PU margarine.

3 Cream yeast with the warm milk. Stir in beaten egg.

4 Pour onto flour mixture and work to a fairly soft dough.

5 Cover with a damp cloth and leave to rise until quantity is doubled.

6 Knead lightly.

7 Turn onto floured board and roll into a rectangle.

8 Brush with melted PU margarine.

9 Sprinkle with currants and mixed spice.

10 Roll up tightly from long side.

11 Brush with remainder of melted margarine.

12 Cut into 1 in. thick slices.

13 Place close together on greased baking sheet or shallow square cake tin, cut sides uppermost.
14 Cover with greased polythene sheet and leave to prove 10 min.
15 Bake in preheated oven, 425 or 7; 20 to 30 min.
16 Dissolve sugar in water in pan over gentle heat, to make bun wash.
17 Bring to boil. Boil 1 min.
18 Brush over buns immediately they are removed from the oven.

Enough for 9 to 12 buns.
A very small amount of egg yolk in each bun.

Iced Bun Round (yeast mixture)

Dough
7 oz. plain flour
1 oz. soya flour
Pinch salt
½ oz. yeast
2 oz. PU margarine
2 oz. caster sugar
4 oz. skimmed milk (scant ¼ pint)
1 egg white

Filling
¾ oz. softened PU margarine
2 oz. caster sugar
1 oz raisins
1 tsp. ground cinnamon

Topping
Glacé icing (page 112)
Cherries and walnut halves for decoration

1 Sieve flour, soya flour and salt into mixing bowl.
2 Heat milk to blood heat, add yeast and PU margarine. Stir until dissolved.
3 Add sugar and lightly beaten egg white.
4 Pour liquid onto flour, mix until smooth and dough leaves the sides of the bowl.
5 Place in large greased polythene bag. Tie bag at top. Leave in a warm place to rise, approx. 45 min.
6 Turn onto floured board and roll to an oblong.

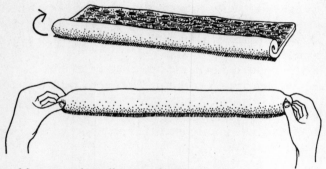

Iced bun round—rolling up dough

7 Spread with softened PU margarine, sprinkle with caster sugar, raisins and cinnamon.
8 Roll up dough tightly and pinch edges to seal.
9 Place on greased baking tray, with join underneath. Bring ends together to form a ring.
10 Cut two thirds through ring at 1½ in. intervals and turn each section on side. Do not cut through completely to centre of ring.

Iced bun round—preparing the sections

11 Leave to prove 15 min.
12 Bake 400 or 6 until a golden brown, 25 to 30 min.
13 Prepare glacé icing and brush over bun whilst still warm.
14 Decorate with cherries and nuts.

Penny Buns

14 oz. plain flour
2 oz. soya flour
Pinch salt
1 level tsp. mixed spice
½ pint skimmed milk

2 oz. caster sugar
2 egg whites
1 oz. fresh yeast
2 oz. currants
4 oz. PU margarine

Bun Wash   2 oz. caster sugar
           4 tbsps. water

1 Sieve flour, soya flour, salt and mixed spice into warm mixing bowl. Add sugar.
2 Heat the milk to blood temperature.
3 Dissolve yeast in the milk, then add the egg whites. Stir to blend.
4 Melt margarine.
5 Pour milk mixture and margarine on to dry ingredients. Mix with fingers to a fairly soft dough for 5 min.
6 Cover with a damp cloth or piece of plastic film and leave until mixture doubles in size.
7 Turn on to floured board and knead in currants.
8 Divide into sixteen or twenty pieces.
9 Roll into balls using cupped hand on a greased board.
10 Place on greased baking tray or one lined with vegetable parchment. Flatten each bun slightly and brush with skimmed milk.
11 Place small dish of warm water in base of oven.
12 Light oven, 425 or 7.
13 When oven has reached the correct temperature set buns to bake. Approx. 15 min.
14 Dissolve sugar in water in saucepan over low heat. When dissolved bring to boil and boil 1 min.
15 Brush bun wash over buns immediately they are cooked.

Flour varies in the amount of liquid it can absorb. It may be necessary to add a little warm water to the dough at step 5.

A free-standing electric mixer may be used to speed the kneading process.

Chocolate Cake
4 oz. PU margarine
4 oz. caster sugar
Vanilla essence

1 tbsp. golden syrup
5 oz. self-raising flour
1 oz. cocoa
½ tsp. baking powder
½ tsp. bicarbonate of soda
6 fl. oz. skimmed milk (a generous ¼ pint)

1 Cream PU margarine and sugar until light and fluffy.
2 Stir in vanilla essence and golden syrup.
3 Sift dry ingredients together.
4 Add milk and dry ingredients alternately to creamed mixture until a soft batter is formed.
5 Turn mixture into a greased 6 in. cake tin.
6 Bake 350 or 4; 45 min. to 1 hour.
7 Leave to cool slightly in tin and the turn out on to a clean tea cloth and then on to a wire rack, so that top of cake is unmarked.

For an attractive finish, place a paper d'oyley on top of cake and sift icing sugar over. Remove d'oyley gently and lo, on top of the cake, a lacy white pattern!

Chocolate and Walnut Gâteau
2 oz. PU margarine
3½ oz. soft brown sugar
4 fl. oz. (scant ¼ pint) buttermilk (made from skimmed milk)
1 egg
4 oz. plain flour
Pinch salt
½ level tsp. bicarbonate of soda
½ level tsp. baking powder
¼ level tsp. ground nutmeg
3 oz. finely chopped walnuts
4 oz. grated chocolate
½ tsp. vanilla essence
Walnut halves and cherries for decoration
Orange icing (see page 112)

1 Grease two 7 in. sandwich tins. Line base with greased greaseproof paper.
2 Cream margarine and sugar.

3 Stir in buttermilk, beaten egg and vanilla essence.
4 Sieve flour, bicarbonate of soda, baking powder, nutmeg and salt onto mixture. Fold in.
5 Add nuts and chocolate. Stir mixture to blend.
6 Divide mixture between the tins.
7 Bake in a preheated oven, 375 or 5; 20 to 25 min.
8 Turn onto wire rack. Remove lining paper.

Sandwich the cooled cakes together with the orange icing. Spread top with the same icing and decorate with walnut halves and cherries. Alternatively fill with cherry pie filling and pipe rosettes of orange icing on top.

One egg yolk in this recipe which will serve eight.

Fruit Cake

8 oz. self-raising flour
3 oz. soft brown sugar
10 oz. mixed dried fruit
½ tsp. grated nutmeg
4 oz. PU margarine
¼ pint skimmed milk
Rind and juice of 1 lemon
1 level tsp. bicarbonate of soda
1 level tbsp. hot water

1 Sieve flour and nutmeg into bowl.
2 Rub in margarine gently.
3 Add milk and stir.
4 Dissolve bicarbonate of soda in hot water and add to mixture with lemon rind and juice.
5 Stir in dried fruit and sugar.
6 Turn into greased and lined 7 in. cake tin.
7 Bake 350 or 4. Approx. 1½ hr.

Bicarbonate of soda is bitter. When used as a raising agent in place of eggs, the flavour of the cake must be strong and definite. Chocolate cake and ginger cake are suitable mixtures.

Lemon Frost Cake

10 oz. self-raising flour
6 oz. PU margarine
6 egg whites

5 oz. icing sugar
2 tbsps. lemon juice
1 tbsp. apricot jam

Topping
1 level tbsp. PU margarine
8 oz. caster sugar
5 tbsps. skimmed milk
1 oz. cocoa powder
$\frac{1}{2}$ tsp. vanilla
Pinch salt

Lemon confectionery slices for decoration.

1 Sieve flour into mixing bowl. Rub in margarine to breadcrumb stage.
2 Whisk egg whites until stiff and dry.
3 Sieve icing sugar onto beaten egg whites and continue whisking until very stiff.
4 Add lemon juice to flour mixture. Stir in meringue.
5 Divide between two greased 8 in. sandwich tins.
6 Bake in preheated oven, 350 or 4. Approx. 20 min.
7 Turn out and leave to cool.
8 Sandwich cakes together with apricot jam.
9 Place milk, caster sugar, cocoa, salt and vanilla in pan. Bring to boil stirring constantly. When boiling point is reached, boil rapidly to soft ball stage. Mixture will seem to thicken and bubbles become larger. Beat in PU margarine.
10 Leave a few moments to cool and thicken.
11 Stand cake on wire rack.
12 Pour icing over cake, lightly tapping rack to spread smoothly.
13 Decorate with sugared lemon jelly slices before icing is set.

Test for soft ball stage (235°F.). A little dropped into a glass of cold water will form a soft ball.

Linzer Torte

4 oz. caster sugar
4 oz. plain flour
4 oz. ground almonds
4 oz. PU margarine

Pinch cinnamon
Pinch salt
½ to 1 egg
½ lb. raspberry jam

1 Mix dry ingredients together.
2 Cut in margarine and rub in.
3 Add sufficient beaten egg to bind into a manageable dough.
4 Chill.
5 Divide dough into two pieces, one slightly larger than the other.
6 Roll large piece ¼ to ½ in. thick into an oblong.
7 Warm jam and spread over paste.
8 Roll out small piece of paste and form strips to make lattice over jammed base.
9 Indent lattice strips with side of finger to give woven appearance.
10 Brush over with remainder of beaten egg.
11 Bake 375 or 5, about 30 min, middle or top of oven.
12 Leave to cool before removing from tin.

This pastry can be difficult to roll out. Roll first piece straight onto baking sheet using vegetable parchment as base, and greaseproof paper on top. Roll second piece of paste between two sheets of greaseproof paper, and lift lattice strips gently using long palette knife. Success is then assured.

A delightful Austrian pastry to eat at any time.

One eighth egg per portion.

Linzer Torte

Low Cholesterol Chocolate Éclairs

Paste

Scant ¼ pint water
2 tbsps. PU oil
2 oz. plain flour
2 egg whites
Pinch salt

Filling

1 rounded tbsp. cornflour
1 level tbsp. caster sugar
¼ pint skimmed milk
¼ tsp. vanilla essence
Yellow colouring

Topping

2 oz. cooking chocolate

1 Light oven, 400 or 6.
2 Place water in small saucepan with oil and salt.
3 Bring to boil, and when boiling fast, toss flour into pan, switch off heat and stir vigorously. The mixture should form a ball which leaves the sides of the pan.
4 Leave to cool a little. Beat in egg whites singly.
5 Place mixture into forcing bag fitted with ½ in. plain nozzle. Pipe mixture on to greased baking tray in 3 in. lengths.
6 Bake near top of oven, 20 to 30 min. Do not open oven for 20 min. or mixture may sink.
7 When well risen and crisp, remove from oven and cut éclairs in half horizontally. Leave to cool.

Filling

1 Blend cornflour, sugar and vanilla essence with the cold milk.
2 Turn into saucepan and bring to boil over low heat stirring constantly. Simmer 2 min.
3 Add colouring.
4 Leave to cool.

To Assemble

1 Spoon the filling into the bottom halves of the éclair shells.
2 Place chocolate on plate over pan of hot water. Switch off heat and leave to melt.

3 Dip rounded tops of éclair halves in chocolate. Place on filled halves.
4 Serve when chocolate has hardened.

For chocolate puffs the mixture may be spooned onto greased baking tray.

Madeleines
Regular Recipe
4 oz. self-raising flour
Pinch baking powder
4 oz. margarine
4 oz. caster sugar
2 large eggs
3 tbsps. sieved apricot jam
6 glacé cherries
4 tbsps. dessicated coconut

Low cholesterol recipe
3 oz. self-raising flour
1 oz. soya flour
Pinch baking powder
4 oz. PU margarine
4 oz. caster sugar
3 egg whites
3 tbsps. sieved apricot jam
6 glacé cherries
2 tbsps. ground almonds
2 tbsps. finely chopped walnuts

1 Light the oven, 350 or 4.
2 Grease ten or twelve dariole moulds.
3 Cream the PU margarine and sugar until light and fluffy.
4 Sieve flour (soya flour) and baking powder.
5 Beat the eggs lightly.
6 Stir the eggs gradually into the creamed mixture.
7 Fold in the flour.
8 Divide mixture between moulds.
9 Bake 15 to 20 min. Turn out on to a wire rack to cool.
10 Warm the jam. Insert the prongs of a fork into the base of the madeleine, and brush top and sides with jam.
11 Spread coconut or mixed nuts on a sheet of greaseproof paper.

12 Still supporting madeleine with the fork, roll in nuts to coat.
13 Halve the cherries and press one on top of each cake.

The mixture may be baked in bun or patty tins but will not look as attractive.

The flour, fat, sugar and eggs in the proportions as given above form the basic ingredients for a wide variety of cakes made by the creaming method. Fairy cakes, queen cakes, walnut cakes, chocolate cakes, cherry cakes, madeira cake and victoria sandwich are all based on this mixture.

Peach Almond Tart

3 oz. caster sugar
5 oz. PU margarine
1 egg
2 oz. ground almonds
Rind of 1 lemon
7 oz. self-raising flour
Peach conserve

1 Cream PU margarine and sugar.
2 Add beaten egg, ground almonds, grated lemon rind and flour.
3 Place half mixture in a forcing bag with star nozzle.
4 Spread remaining half mixture evenly in base of 7 in. sandwich tin.
5 Pipe deep rosettes of mixture around edge of base.
6 Spoon 2 tbsps. peach conserve in centre.
7 Bake at 375 or 5; 30 min.
8 Serve cold.

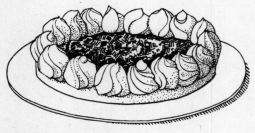

Peach almond tart

A substantial 'torte' which will serve eight. About one eighth egg per person.

This is a dessert to make when your wrists are strong as the mixture is rather solid and requires pressure on forcing bag. The jam will spread during baking and set into a thick jelly when cold. Either serve from the tin or remove when completely cold.

Brandy Snaps

2 oz. PU margarine
2 oz. caster sugar
2 level tbsps. golden syrup
2 oz. plain flour
½ level tsp. ground ginger
1 tsp. brandy
Grated rind of ½ lemon
1 tsp. lemon juice

1 Light oven, 350 or 4
2 Melt margarine, sugar and syrup over low heat.
3 Switch off heat. Stir in flour and ginger.
4 Add brandy, lemon rind and juice. Mix well.
5 Leave to cool, 1 to 2 min.
6 Line three baking sheets with vegetable parchment.
7 Place teaspoonsful of mixture 4 in. apart on tins about three per tin.
8 Place one tin in top of oven and bake 7 to 10 min. until golden and bubbly.
9 Immediately first batch is cooked remove from oven and put in next batch.
10 Wait 30 sec. and when beginning to set roll around greased handles of wooden spoons. Leave until set and gently twist off.

If biscuits set too hard before rolling, they can be returned to the oven for a few moments to soften.

You will need at least three wooden spoons, and they must be well oiled.

Brandy snaps can be stored in a tin for one week.

Vegetable parchment which looks like but is NOT grease-proof paper may be used whenever a mixture is likely to stick or whenever you would like to avoid washing up a sticky baking tin. It is available at stationers and is not expensive as, provided the oven is not too hot, it can be washed and used again and again.

Dentelles
2 egg whites
4 oz. caster sugar
2 oz. plain flour
½ tsp. vanilla essence
1 oz. blanched shredded almonds
2 oz. PU margarine

1 Melt PU margarine. Set aside to cool.
2 Break egg whites into a bowl. Whisk until stiff.
3 Add just under half the sugar and whisk again until meringue forms 'peaks'.
4 Fold in remainder of sugar.
5 Sieve flour over meringue and fold in gently.
6 Add vanilla and almonds.
7 Mix in cooled margarine.
8 Place teaspoonsful of mixture well spaced out on baking tray lined with vegetable parchment.
9 Bake 375 or 5 until golden brown. Approx. 15 min.
10 When cooked, lift off baking tray carefully and lay over rolling pin to cool. Press biscuits against pin with palm of hand to form curve while still hot.

If biscuits harden too quickly, return to oven for a few seconds.

As the French name suggests, the biscuits should be as thin as lace.

Flapjacks
3 oz. PU margarine
4 level tbsps. golden syrup
3 oz. demerara sugar
5 oz. porridge oats

1 Grease a 7 in. square shallow tin. (It is necessary to grease even if you have a non-stick pan.)
2 Melt margarine, syrup and sugar in pan over low heat, stirring all the time.

3 Stir in porridge oats and turn into prepared tin.
4 Flatten mixture evenly with palette knife.
5 Bake in centre of oven, 350 or 4; 25 min.
6 Leave to cool a little, then mark in squares. Turn out when cold.

Flapjacks are usually recommended as a first recipe for child-cooks.

Always successful. These biscuits should be stored in an airtight container.

Macaroon Biscuits
2 oz. ground almonds
½ oz. ground rice
3 oz. caster sugar
1 egg white (from a large egg)
¼ tsp. vanilla essence
Blanched almonds or almond flakes to decorate
Rice paper

1 Mix ground almonds, ground rice and sugar in mixing bowl.
2 Add vanilla essence to egg white and beat until frothy.
3 Add egg mixture to dry ingredients and mix with a fork to a fairly stiff consistency.
4 Line two baking trays with rice paper, shiny side up.
5 Divide mixture into 9 to 12 pieces and roll into balls with the palms of the hands dusted lightly with icing sugar.
6 Place balls well spread out on rice paper, and flatten slightly with palette knife.
7 Put a blanched almond in the centre of each biscuit.
8 Bake 350 or 4; 25 min. until they are a pale brown colour.
9 Slide fish slice under rice paper to loosen biscuits and place on wire rack to cool.
10 Surplus rice paper will break away easily when the biscuits are cold.

Macaroons may be baked on vegetable parchment if you do not like rice paper, or if it is difficult to obtain.

Viennese Biscuits

6 oz. PU margarine
2 oz. caster sugar
6 oz. plain flour
½ tsp. vanilla essence
2 or 3 chopped glacé cherries

1 Cream PU margarine and sugar until light and fluffy.
2 Stir in vanilla essence.
3 Stir in flour.
4 Place mixture in forcing bag fitted with large star nozzle.
5 Pipe round and 'S' shapes on to baking sheet.
6 Decorate with chopped cherries.
7 Bake 350 or 4; 20 to 25 min.

12. Egg yolks
for the others

An egg yolk is 30% of the total weight of the whole egg. Almost the entire fat content of the egg is in the yolk. An average egg yolk contains 6 gm. of fat, 4.8% of which is cholesterol, and useful quantities of Vitamin A, Vitamin D, Vitamin B_2 and iron. All flavour is concentrated in the egg yolk. An egg yolk solidifies at 150°F., so that there is no need to cook eggs in boiling water.

Egg yolks may be poached, i.e. placed in simmering water until they are soft or cooked a little longer until they become hard. They can also be put in a greased china egg cup and covered with foil. The egg cup is then placed in a saucepan of very hot water reaching halfway up the cup and left to 'coddle'.

Additional hard egg yolks can always be included with other whole hard boiled eggs chopped up for sandwich fillings, or raw yolks with other eggs for omelettes and scrambled eggs. If you are making a risotto, garnish with chopped or sieved hard boiled yolks.

Although whole eggs are normally used for binding, the surplus yolks can be used for binding duchesse potatoes, rissoles or stuffing. When coating foods to be fried, an extra yolk can be added to the whole egg. On the other hand, yolks on their own produce a better texture than do whole eggs for thickening custards and sauces. An egg yolk can be used in place of flour or cornflour for thickening gravy, but make sure the temperature is only warm when adding the egg yolk and heat slowly.

An additional egg yolk will make the batter richer **for**

yorkshire pudding, pancakes and the like, and in mayonnaise an extra yolk will strengthen the emulsion.

In order to create a rich brown gloss to pies, pastries and biscuits, beat an egg yolk with a teaspoon of water and brush this mixture on the top surface before baking in the oven. And when making pastry a little of the milk or water in the mixture may be omitted and replaced with an egg yolk.

Apricot Tartlets

2 oz. plain flour
Pinch salt
1 oz. caster sugar
1¼ oz. butter
1 egg yolk
2 oz. plain chocolate
1 can apricot halves
1 level tsp. arrowroot
¼ pint syrup

1 Soften the butter at room temperature.
2 Sieve flour and salt onto worktop.
3 Rub in butter.
4 Add sugar.
5 Sprinkle beaten egg yolk over mixture, gradually draw in from sides to centre until well mixed.
6 Cover and place in refrigerator.
7 Grease nine bun or patty tins.
8 Roll out pastry, cut into rounds and line tins. Prick well.
9 Bake 375 or 5; 10 min.
10 Remove from tins and leave to cool.
11 Drain apricots and retain syrup.
12 Melt chocolate on plate over hot water.
13 Place one apricot half, round side up, in each pastry case.
14 Stir arrowroot into ¼ pint of syrup. Place in saucepan and bring to boil to thicken, stirring constantly. When sauce clears, it is ready.
15 Coat apricots with sauce.
16 Dip bottoms of tartlets into chocolate and leave on waxed paper until set.

If pastry is difficult to roll out, it has been under refrigeration for insufficient time.

Heart watchers may occasionally eat these tartlets if they are prepared with PU margarine. Each tartlet has 1/9th egg yolk.

Crème au Caramel

Caramel
3 oz. sugar
¼ pt. (5 fl. oz.) water

Custard
½ pint milk
4 egg yolks
1 oz. caster sugar
½ tsp. vanilla essence

1 Dissolve 3 oz. sugar in water, slowly bring to boil and allow to bubble unstirred until syrup turns brown.
2 Quickly pour into hot ovenproof mould (1 pint). Leave until cold.
3 Heat milk, but do not boil.
4 Stir in 1 oz. caster sugar and vanilla essence.
5 Pour on to slightly beaten egg yolks.
6 Strain mixture into prepared mould.
7 Cover with greased greaseproof paper and stand in roasting tin half filled with warm water.
8 Bake in oven 350 or 4; 1 to 1½ hr.
9 Leave to cool or refrigerate before turning out onto serving dish.

Crème au caramel may be cooked successfully in a pressure cooker. Place ½ pint water in pressure pan, cover mould with foil and stand on trivet. Bring to pressure of 15 lb. and cook 4 min. Switch off heat and allow to cool naturally.

Many people are afraid of pressure cookers imagining that they frequently 'blow-up'. If properly used and directions followed, they are perfectly safe and save two thirds of normal cooking time.

Crème Patissière

6 oz. caster sugar
5 egg yolks
Scant 3 oz. plain flour
¾ pint milk
½ oz. butter
Vanilla essence

1 Whisk egg yolks and sugar in a bowl over a saucepan of hot water until the mixture thickens to the consistency of half-whipped cream.
2 Add the flour.
3 Heat the milk until hot but not boiling.
4 Gradually add the hot milk to the egg mixture beating all the time.
5 Strain the mixture back into the saucepan, add vanilla essence and bring slowly to the boil. Stir continuously. When the sauce thickens, beat vigorously.
6 Remove from heat and add butter.
7 Turn into a bowl and cover with a wet piece of grease-proof paper, the wet side against the surface of the custard.

Crème Pattissière is a superior custard used as a filling for éclairs and french pastries such as milles feuilles. A fruit flan is vastly improved if a layer of this custard is spread on the cooked pastry before adding the fruit.

Custard Sauce

½ pint whole milk
2 egg yolks
1 oz sugar
1 piece of thinly pared lemon rind

1 Place milk in saucepan with lemon rind. Heat but do not boil.
2 Beat egg yolks. Add milk stirring constantly.
3 Strain mixture back into the saucepan, add the sugar and cook over a very low heat until the sauce thickens sufficiently to form a translucent covering on the spoon.

Should you lack confidence, the custard may be thickened in the top section of a double saucepan over simmering water.

The above proportions are for a thin sauce. Use 4 egg yolks for a thick custard.

Egg croquettes
4 egg yolks
½ oz. butter
½ oz. flour
⅛ pint vegetable stock
Salt and pepper
1 tbsp. beaten egg

Coating   Beaten egg and breadcrumbs.

1 Poach the egg yolks in water at simmering point until hard. Approx. 5 min.
2 Drain. Allow to cool. Chop finely.
3 Melt the butter in a small saucepan. Add the flour and blend in the vegetable stock. Season to taste.
4 Bring slowly to boil until the sauce thickens. Remove from heat.
5 Mix the chopped egg yolks with the sauce. Add beaten egg and return to heat to set the mixture.
6 Turn onto a wet plate to prevent the mixture from sticking and leave to cool. Cover with damp greaseproof paper.
7 When cold, divide mixture into four. Shape into croquettes with floured hands.
8 Dip into beaten egg and coat with breadcrumbs.
9 Repeat this process pressing crumbs well in with a palette knife.
10 Fry in hot deep or shallow fat.

Serve with ¼ pint of cheese sauce at pouring consistency.
One egg should be enough for binding and coating in this recipe.

Hollandaise Sauce
6 oz. unsalted butter
3 egg yolks
1 tbsp. lemon juice
1 tbsp. water
Pinch salt
Pinch cayenne

1 Place egg yolks, salt and cayenne in fireproof glass bowl over saucepan of hot water.
2 Whisk vigorously with rotary beater or balloon whisk.
3 Add lemon juice and water. Beat thoroughly until sauce thickens.
4 Remove bowl from saucepan. Whisk in butter in small pats until it is all incorporated and sauce has consistency of whipped double cream.

At end of step 3 a teaspoonful of the mixture dropped on to its surface should remain for a few moments before sinking in.

If mixture curdles through overheating, remove from heat and stir in 1 tbsp. hot water.

Lemon Curd
8 oz. unsalted butter
8 egg yolks
6 lemons
1 lb. granulated sugar

1 Scrub lemons and grate rind finely.
2 Squeeze out juice.
3 One third fill base of double saucepan with boiling water. Place over low heat.
4 Place butter in top saucepan and melt.
5 Stir in sugar, lemon juice and rind, and allow sugar to dissolve.
6 Break up egg yolks in basin.
7 Pour on lemon mixture, stir and strain back into top saucepan.
8 Stir constantly over simmering water until mixture thickens. Approx. 5 min.
9 Remove from heat when pouring consistency reached, and pot in warm jars.

The mixture will fill about three 1 lb. jars. It will keep 2 or 3 weeks. Home made lemon curd potted in small attractive jars makes a gift that is different.

If you do not have a double saucepan, use two saucepans. One should be slightly smaller than the other to allow it to fit comfortably without tipping over. The water must not touch the bottom of the upper pan.

Raspberry Bavarois

1 pint whole milk
4 oz. caster sugar
4 egg yolks
8 oz. frozen raspberries
½ pint half-whipped double cream
1 oz. gelatine
¼ pint hot water
Red vegetable colouring

1 Spread the raspberries on absorbent kitchen paper until thawed.
2 Lightly break up the egg yolks with a fork and blend with a little of the milk.
3 Bring the remainder of the milk and sugar slowly to the boil.
4 Switch off heat. Add egg mixture to saucepan and whisk thoroughly.
5 Dissolve gelatine in the water. Pour from a height onto sauce and mix thoroughly.
6 Press raspberries through a sieve into a mixing bowl. Rinse the strainer.
7 Pass sauce while still warm through the strainer onto the raspberry pulp. Stir. Add colouring.
8 When cool, but not set, stir in half-whipped cream.
9 Rinse mould in cold water, shake out surplus and fill with raspberry mixture. Leave to set.

Dip moulds in hot water for a few seconds before turning out.

Cream and all utensils should be cold for whipping. A hand operated rotary beater best allows the cook to whip the cream to the desired consistency. To half-whip cream, beat until a spoonful dropped on the surface will stay a few moments before sinking in. Fully whipped cream will stand up in peaks.

Over-whipped cream causes the whey to separate.

Refrigerated Gâteau Fletton

1½ packets sponge finger biscuits
1 tbsp. rum
3 oz. plain chocolate

6 oz. caster sugar
6 oz. unsalted butter
1 egg yolk
3 glacé cherries

1 Grease and line an 8 in. square or 1 lb. loaf tin.
2 Melt chocolate in a bowl over hot water.
3 Add butter and sugar and stir until dissolved.
4 Add egg yolk. Blend thoroughly.
5 Dip biscuits in rum and fit a layer into base of tin.
6 Cover with a layer of sauce.
7 Continue layering biscuits and sauce alternately.
8 Cover with a sheet of polythene or piece of foil.
9 Put a heavy weight on top.
10 Leave in refrigerator until set; 2 or 3 hr.
11 Turn onto cake dish and decorate with glacé cherries.

Spread a little jam on cut halves of glacé cherries to keep them in place on gâteau.

Keep the gâteau in the refrigerator as the chocolate softens if left in a warm room.

Sauce Béarnaise (1)
½ pint béchamel sauce (page 115)
1 onion, chopped
2 tbsps. malt vinegar
2 tbsps. tarragon vinegar
1 level tsp. chopped parsley
2 egg yolks

1 Place vinegars in saucepan, add onion and parsley and simmer until reduced. The liquid should then measure 1 tbsp.
2 Place béchamel sauce in top half of double saucepan, having boiling water in the base.
3 Strain vinegar onto sauce.
4 Switch on heat, add egg yolks. Stir until sauce is hot but not boiling. Remove 'threads' from egg yolks before adding to sauce.

Sauce Béarnaise (2)

4 tbsps. tarragon vinegar
10 crushed peppercorns
2 level tsps. shallots, finely chopped
1 tbsp. water
4 or 5 egg yolks
8 oz. melted unsalted butter
Juice of ½ lemon
Salt
Cayenne pepper
1 level tsp. chopped chervil, fresh or dried.

1 Place vinegar, peppercorns and shallots in saucepan. Simmer until reduced by half.
2 Leave to cool a little. Add water and egg yolks.
3 Transfer mixture into top of double saucepan or fit saucepan over another suitable pan, half filled with hot water.
4 Cook over low heat, whisking all the time.
5 When mixture thickens, whisk in butter gradually.
6 Add lemon juice, salt and cayenne to taste.
7 Strain into warmed jug.
8 Sprinkle with chervil.

Sauce Béarnaise is served with red meats and is a derivative of Sauce Hollandaise.

Sauce Gribiche

1 hard boiled whole egg
1 hard boiled egg yolk
1 raw egg yolk
½ pint olive oil
Juice and rind of ½ lemon
1 tsp. french mustard
1 tsp. salt
Pinch pepper
2 tsps. gherkins, chopped
2 tsps capers, chopped
1 tsp. parsley, chopped

1 Pound the two hard boiled egg yolks with 1 tsp. lemon juice.

2 Add raw egg yolk (threads removed), mustard, salt and pepper. Beat well.
3 Whisk in oil drop by drop at room temperature until mayonnaise is thick.
4 Stir in remaining lemon juice, lemon rind, gherkins, capers, parsley and chopped egg white.

Sauce Poissonière

1½ oz. butter
1½ oz. flour
¼ pint milk
½ pint fish stock
2 egg yolks
¼ pint cream
1 or 2 tsps. lemon juice
Salt and pepper

1 Melt the butter in a saucepan over low heat, blend in flour and cook 1 min.
2 Stir in stock and milk, bring to boil stirring all the time. Cook 2 min.
3 Blend egg yolks with the cream.
4 Beat sauce into egg mixture a teaspoonful at a time.
5 Add lemon juice, salt and pepper.
6 Return mixture to saucepan and gradually bring to boil.

Serve with hot steamed, grilled or baked fish.

Savoury Mousseline Sauce

2 egg yolks
⅛ pint (2½ fl. oz.) cream
1 tbsp. chicken stock
½ oz. butter
Lemon juice
Salt, pepper, nutmeg

1 Place egg yolks, cream and stock in saucepan.
2 Whisk over gentle heat until well mixed and thickened.
3 Whisk in butter in small pats.
4 Add lemon juice, salt, pepper and nutmeg to taste.
5 Serve at once.

Whisking will take about 7 min.
Serve mousseline sauce with fish.

Vanilla Ice Cream

2 pints whole milk
6 egg yolks
½ tsp. vanilla essence
8 oz. caster sugar

1 Place milk, sugar and vanilla in a saucepan and bring to boil over gentle heat.
2 Beat egg yolks in large mixing bowl.
3 Gradually add the milk mixture whisking continuously. Allow mixture to rest for 5 min.
4 Whisk again and strain into freezer container or ice-cream machine.
5 Place in the freezer or the freezer compartment of the refrigerator set at cold.
6 When ice cream is half set, whisk again and return to freezer.

Zabaglione

¼ pint (5 fl.oz.) marsala
3 tbsps. white wine
1½ oz. caster sugar
4 egg yolks

1 Place sugar and egg yolks in bowl over pan of hot but not boiling water.
2 Whisk vigorously until mixture fluffs up and thickens.
3 Gradually whisk in marsala and white wine until mixture is very thick.

Serve with sponge finger biscuits.
If possible use an electric beater to give a larger volume and speed the process. It can take up to 15 minutes if whisked by hand.
Make sure the mixing bowl does not tip off the saucepan.

Zuppa Pavese

2 pints chicken stock
½ pint water
1 onion, chopped
1 carrot, chopped
Bouquet garni

Salt and pepper
1 slice french bread, crusts removed ⎫
½ oz. parmesan cheese, grated   ⎬ per person
1 raw egg yolk   ⎭

1 Cook onion and carrot in chicken stock and water, with bouquet garni, salt and pepper until tender. Taste, adjust seasoning.
2 Remove bouquet garni, continue to simmer soup while toasting the bread.
3 Pour the hot soup into individual bowls. Drop in egg yolk so that it is completely immersed.
4 Push yolk to one side of bowl and add toast sprinkled with cheese.
5 Serve at once. The yolk should remain runny.

13 How to . . .

In this chapter you will find detailed instructions for some of the processes mentioned in various recipes. There are also some additional hints and tips included that may be of interest in cookery generally. As they are not all in their strict alphabetical order, here is a list of the contents of this chapter:

How to bone a chicken whole and uncooked
1 Lay chicken on its back.
2 Remove wings at second joint.
3 Cut off drumsticks completely.
4 Turn chicken over so that breast is underneath.
5 Use sharp knife to slit down back skin.
6 Fillet off back flesh with flat of knife, leaving the skin intact through whole of process.
7 Fillet around rib cage.
8 Fillet around thigh bone.
9 Turn leg inside out and fillet off meat.
10 Fillet around wing. Tuck in.
11 Repeat other side. Remove parsons nose.
12 Fillet breast while still underneath, holding carcase in hand.
13 Leave thighs tucked in. Remove sinews with scissors.
14 Remove blood clots with damp muslin.

If you are right handed, always fillet towards the left, turning the chicken when necessary.

How to joint a chicken the easy way
1 Rest the chicken on a chopping board breast uppermost and the neck end towards you.
2 Remove leg and wing tips up to the first joint of each.
3 Cut the breast along the line of the breast bone with secateurs or kitchen scissors. This permits the upper section of the chicken to open slightly.
4 Insert in that opening a long sharp knife and hit each end of the blade with the flat end of a rolling pin to cut the carcase in two.
5 Lay one half on a chopping board skin side up. Stretch the piece to separate the wing from the leg and cut through the flesh in the centre.

6 Repeat for other half.
7 To make eight pieces divide each quarter in half across the bone.

How to prepare fish

The fishmonger will usually fillet the fish if requested. Some fish such as plaice are often sold in fillets, and the cost per edible portion is the same whether purchased as fillets or on the bone. Round fish is sold in cutlets or fillets. Haddock and cod are the most readily available.

To fillet flat fish

1 Remove head and wash cavity under cold running water. Rub salt onto blood clots and rinse thoroughly.
2 Lay fish on chopping board with tail towards you.
3 Cut down centre of fish to backbone.
4 With sharp flexible knife, cut along backbone towards sides, working from centre to left.
5 Turn fish round and remove second fillet.
6 Turn fish over and repeat with other two fillets.

To skin flat fish

1 Lay fillet on board, skin side underneath.
2 Dip thumb and forefinger of one hand in salt and hold tail firmly against edge of board.
3 Remove flesh by pressing and sawing with sharp knife from tail to head, keeping knife as flat as possible.

To fillet round fish

1 Cut down the centre of the back as far as the bone.
2 Slit open along belly flap.
3 Using a sharp knife, work along bone from head to tail using short strokes. The bone should be underneath the flesh.

To skin round fish

1 Cut through skin beneath head.
2 Dip fingertips in salt and pull skin off from head to tail on one side.
3 Turn on to other side and repeat.

To fillet herrings
1 Remove head and entrails.
2 Wash under running cold water and cleanse cavity with salt.
3 Slip a knife under belly flap and cut through to reveal bone.
4 Open flaps with both hands and hold on board, bone downwards.
5 Press through backbone with knuckles until fish flattens.
6 Reverse fish and lift off bone.

To fillet cooked Dover sole
1 Working from backbone to sides, insert prongs of a fork between bones and push flesh away from centre. Steady the fish with a tablespoon held firmly against back bone.
2 Discard skeleton. Trim away fine bones at sides.

Points to note when deep fat frying
The pan should be not more than one third full.

The average temperature should be 375°F. When the fat is as hot as this, the surface of the food will seal at once and so avoid oil penetration. At low temperatures the flavour of the food permeates the oil and makes it unsuitable for frying foods of different flavours.

At the correct frying temperature food should rise immediately to the surface. The oil is too cool if food rests on the bottom of the pan and too hot if bubbles are seen around it.

If no thermometer is available, drop a cube of white bread into the hot oil. It should take 20 sec. to turn golden brown. If the bread remains pale, the oil is not hot enough, but if it turns dark brown, the oil is too hot.

Overheated oil burns particles of food causing rancidity. The oil cannot then be reused.

Oil may be strained and re-used but every time it is reheated a certain amount of hydrogenation takes place, thus diminishing the cholesterol reducing qualities of the linoleic acid.

Doughnuts, fritters and fish should be fried at 360–375°F; reheated foods, rissoles, fish cakes, croquette potatoes, etc. 375°F. and chipped potatoes 375–380°F. Temperatures between 360°F and 380°F are generally acceptable.

Food may be raw and uncoated, coated with batter or egg and bread crumbs or egg white and breadcrumbs.

Uncoated raw foods should be dry before frying.

Chipped Potatoes
1 Place in frying basket.
2 Bring oil to 375°F.
3 Lower basket into oil and cook until chips are tender.
4 Lift basket and rest on side of pan to allow oil to reheat.
5 Return basket to oil to complete frying. Drain and serve.

Have a fitting saucepan lid ready in case of fire.

In the event of the oil setting fire in the pan, switch off heat and place lid on pan. Should food cause oil to boil over and set fire, switch off heat, leave pan on cooker, close doors and windows and wait for fire to die down.

It is possible to buy an aerosol fire extinguisher to keep in case of emergency.

How to make a bouquet garni
A bouquet garni is a bunch of herbs, fresh or dried, placed in a square of muslin and tied to form a little bag. The herbs can then be easily removed from sauces, soups or stews before serving. The herbs should consist of parsley, thyme and bay leaves.

How to deal with garlic
Many people are apprehensive of using garlic. This is a great pity since garlic improves the flavour of many dishes. However, only a very small amount should be used, and in tiny quantities the taste of garlic is not detectable.

Garlic is obtainable at most greengrocers and is sold by the 'head'. This is made up of several 'cloves', each enclosed in several thin skins.

Pull a clove of garlic from the head, peel and crush in a garlic press or place between sheets of greaseproof paper and flatten with a cleaver. The garlic can then be removed and the paper thrown away, leaving no smell on the chopping board. If you propose to use a can of food, crush the garlic with its base before opening the can.

Garlic is now available in powder form which keeps very well. A squeeze is enough for most dishes.

Garnishes
Soups are often made more attractive by the addition of a garnish. This may be chopped parsley, strips of pancakes, small puffs of baked choux paste, croutons or julienne strips.

To make julienne strips
1 Peel vegetables and cut into $\frac{1}{8}$ in. thick slices.
2 Cut these into strips about 2 in. long to resemble match sticks.
3 Blanch for 1 or 2 min. and drain.
4 Add to hot soup.

Carrots, turnips, leeks and celery are the vegetables normally used. Allow $\frac{1}{4}$ oz. per serving.

Restaurant menus often given elaborate descriptions. Jardiniere are thicker strips, macedoines are large dice, and brunoise tiny diced vegetables. These garnishes may be tossed in butter.

To make citrus fruit garnishes
1 Pare the thin skin from oranges, lemons or grapefruit.
2 Cut into julienne strips.
3 Blanch 5 to 10 min. until tender. Drain.
4 Moisten with stock syrup and use as a garnish for fruit salads, and open fruit flans.

Lemon garnishes
In addition to enhancing the appearance of a dish, lemons add a piquancy to the flavour and supply vitamin C. The pips should always be removed.

Lemon wedges
1 Wash and dry the lemon.
2 Cut in half lengthways.
3 Divide each half into three lengthways.

Each lemon provides 6 wedges which may not be sufficiently economical.

Lemon butterflies
1 Wash and dry the lemon.
3 Slice thinly crosswise to obtain rounds.

3 Using a sharp knife, remove a small triangle from two opposite sides. The point of the knife should just reach the centre pith.

Lemon butterflies

One lemon is enough for 10 or 12 thin butterflies.

Lemon Twists
1 Wash and dry the lemon.
2 Slice thinly crosswise to obtain rounds.
3 Lay each round flat on a board and make one cut from the centre pith to the edge.
4 Just before serving, twist the lemon slice and stand it upright, so that one side of the incision is facing forwards and the other backwards.

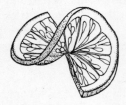

Lemon twists

One lemon is enough for 8 to 10 twists.

Gelatine
Gelatine is a weak protein which thickens liquids and so forms bulk. This is the reason it is often used in slimmers' recipes for the volume of food is increased without adding any calories.

Gelatine is made either from animal or vegetable matter. The animal gelatine is mostly produced by two well-known manufacturers from purified and processed bones and connective tissue of young animals. Agar-agar is of vegetable origin, coming mainly from seaweed and is obtainable from health food shops. As a rough guide,

$\frac{1}{2}$ oz. animal gelatine sets 1 pint of liquid
$\frac{1}{4}$ oz. agar-agar sets 1 pint of liquid

Remember, however, that more gelatine would be required in hot weather or hotter climates.

Gelatine should be dissolved in liquid that is hot but not boiling, for if the liquid boils the setting power of the gelatine is reduced and an unpleasant flavour develops. The liquid should be placed in a heatproof bowl, the gelatine added and the bowl then stood in a pan of boiling water. Stirring should continue until all the gelatine is dissolved.

When adding the prepared gelatine to food mixtures, the temperature of the gelatine solution should be as close as possible to that of the food to which it is being added. If a hot solution is added to a cold mixture, it will set before integrating and 'rope'.

Gelatine solutions may be used for glazing pies and pastry in place of beaten egg.

Meringue

If you are unsuccessful at producing good meringues, it is probably not your fault. Humidity in the atmosphere is often the ruination of meringues. Keep the kitchen warm and dry, and try to prepare meringues when there are no kettles or saucepans boiling on the hob.

Eggs should be at room temperature and should be a few days old.

All utensils must be free from grease, and eggs should be separated one at a time in small containers before being put in the mixing bowl.

The largest volume of beaten egg white is produced by using a balloon whisk and a copper bowl. However, an ordinary mixing bowl and rotary beater, or electric mixer give adequate speedy results.

Use 2 oz. sugar to each egg white and if possible use an equal quantity of caster and granulated sugar.

Whisk the egg whites until stiff and dry.

Add less than half of the sugar and beat until mixture forms peaks.

Sprinkle the remaining sugar on top and fold in with a metal spoon. Do not stir the mixture which would cause it to collapse.

Meringue Suisse

For ordinary everday meringues. Oil a baking tray or

line it with vegetable parchment. Scoop a heaped dessert-spoonful of mixture with one spoon and remove it onto the tray with the bowl of a second similar spoon to produce smooth shapes.

The mixture may be placed in a forcing bag and piped into any desired shape.

For crisp white meringues, place in a very slow oven 200 or ¼ for 4 hr.

If you prefer a light beige homemade look, crisp outside but 'gooey' inside, bake 275 or 1 for about 1 hr

Meringue Cuite

Made with icing sugar and egg whites. Use at least 2 oz. icing sugar to each large egg white.

Place icing sugar and egg whites in a bowl over a pan of hot water.

Whisk until stiff.

Meringue cuite can easily be prepared in a table model electric mixer. Use the whisk attachment, and beat at high speed. This meringue is easily piped but tends to set rather hard.

Bake at 275 or 1, approx. 45 min.

Meringue Italienne

A good substitute filling for sandwich cakes. A thermometer is needed for correct temperature.

4 oz. cube sugar
3¾ fl. oz. water
2 egg whites
Flavouring and colouring

Boil sugar to 260°F.

Pour onto stiffly beaten egg whites, whisking vigorously. Continue whisking until all sugar is absorbed and mixture is stiff. Flavour and colour as desired.

An electric beater must be used unless you have an assistant to pour the syrup over the egg whites whilst you whisk.

How to use a forcing bag

Forcing bags are used for piping meringues, choux pastry,

potatoes, biscuits, sweet or savoury pastes, cream, icing, etc. They are obtainable in small or large sizes, and are made of cotton, nylon or plastic. Before filling, a nozzle or pipe is dropped into the bag to protrude from the pointed end. The larger nozzles are star shaped or plain, and the smaller pipes are shaped in many different patterns. Some pipes or nozzles have screw fittings, and special rings can be bought to screw the pipes on to the bags. These are not very effective with paper bags.

To fill

1 Stand the bag in an empty jug and turn the top back to form a cuff.
2 Fill the bag with a spoon or palette knife. As the spoon is withdrawn wipe off surplus mixture with the side of the forefinger.
3 Unfold the cuff, remove the bag from the jug and lay sideways on table.
4 Press the side of the hand on the surface of bag, press and push the mixture towards the nozzle.
5 Hold the bag tightly in one hand just above the mixture.
6 Squeeze so as to force the mixture through the nozzle whilst guiding with the other hand.

When piping round shapes such as buns, hold the bag upright $\frac{1}{4}$ in. above the baking tray, raise the nozzle gradually and finish with a sharp downward push.

For long items such as éclairs, the bag should be held at an angle, the nozzle close to the baking tray, and the bag drawn along sideways. Potato borders or similar decorative work are best accomplished when the bag is held with the pipe furthest away from the cook, then drawn towards her.

To increase the height of a decoration, keep the nozzle well away from the surface of the previously piped mixture.

Small pipes are used for piping decorations on cakes, such as rosettes. It is often practicable to make a piping bag from greaseproof paper. This is particularly convenient when only a small quantity of icing is required.

To make a piping bag

1 Fold a 10 in. square of greaseproof paper in half, corner to corner, to form a triangle.

2 Fold over the long edge once more, then open out. The fold from the apex to the centre of the base of the triangle serves as a guide.
3 Grasp one of the lower corners between thumb and forefinger, holding the paper steady at the base of the fold.
4 Turn the corner inwards and curve the paper so that the edge lies along the centre fold and the corner meets the apex.
5 Hold the two points together at the apex and grasp the second lower corner and curve it around the front of the cone to meet the fold at the back making the corners join at the apex. There will be a stiff point at the bottom of the cone.
6 Fold the apex inwards twice to secure the folds.
7 Tear off approx. $\frac{1}{2}$ in. from the bottom of the cone and drop in a small pipe.
8 Fill as previously with mixture but do not overfill.
9 Close top by folding the two sides to the middle first and then fold down top to finally seal.
10 To pipe, grasp from the top with one hand, guiding with the other

Mushrooms
Unless mushrooms are very dirty or stale there is no need to peel them.

1 Wash in clean cold water.
2 Rest the mushrooms sideways on a board.
3 Hold the cap firmly and cut off the stalk level with the edge of the cap.
4 Reserve these stalks for soups or stocks.

Whole mushrooms retain their shape during cooking if the part of the stalk nearest the cap is left attached.

To slice
1 Place round side up on chopping board.
2 Cut downwards with sharp knife.

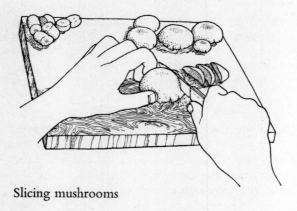

Slicing mushrooms

Nuts

To skin shelled almonds, pistachios, etc
1 Cover nuts with boiling water and leave for a few minutes.
2 Strain.
3 Pressing upwards between the thumb and forefinger will then remove the skins easily.

To skin shelled hazelnuts
1 Lay nuts on a baking tray.
2 Place in a moderate oven 375 or 5.
3 Leave for a few minutes, then remove from oven, and rub in clean teacloth. The skins should come away easily.

To brown hazelnuts
Replace in oven, but hazelnuts burn quickly so cannot be left.

To chop nuts
1 Place nuts close together on a large chopping board.
2 With the thumb and forefinger of the left hand, hold the pointed end of a long kitchen knife firmly against the board cutting edge down.
3 Grip handle of knife with the other hand and chop forwards and backwards over nuts. As nuts scatter, gather them up and repeat.

Chestnuts

To shell and skin
1 Slit the flat side with a sharp knife.
2 Half fill a saucepan with water, add a pinch of salt and bring to boil.
3 Drop the nuts a few at a time into the boiling water, and cook for about 5 min. until the slit begins to open.
4 Remove from water with perforated spoon, dry in a cloth and peel and skin while hot.

An alternative method is to split the shells and bake in a hot oven, 400 or 6, for 5 min. Shell hot.

To cook
Place split nuts all at once in boiling salted water and cook until tender, approx. 30 min. Drain and shell.

Sweet chestnut purée can be made at home by mixing stock syrup with sieved chestnuts, which have been boiled with only a pinch of salt, but canned purée can usually be found in grocers' shops.

There are many canned varieties such as whole chestnuts, sweet chestnut spread, unsweetened chestnut purée (suitable for stuffings) and of course marron glacé.

Onions

To chop
1 Stand onion root end down on chopping board.
2 Cut in half through stalk and root.
3 Pull off outer skin from stalk to root. Do not remove root at this stage.
4 Lay halved onions on board cut side down with the root end next to your left hand (unless you are left-handed).

Cutting onions

5 Hold the root end firmly with the finger tips curved under.

6 Make four or five horizontal cuts from stalk end of the onion to the root end leaving the root intact.

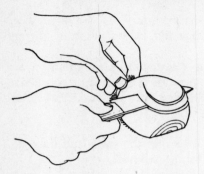

7 Make four or five vertical cuts not quite reaching the root end.

8 Continuing to hold the onion firmly in the same position slice finely holding the knife at right angles to the previous cuts.

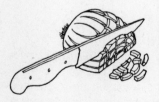

The onion will now fall apart in neat dice and the root end can be discarded. Left-handed cooks should reverse the position of the onion and work from left to right.

Many ways have been suggested to avoid 'tears' but I find it is best to work in small quantities and only peel the onions when required thus avoiding the smell in the kitchen.

To slice

1 Cut onion in half from stalk to root, remove outer skin and hold as previously shown.
2 Cut slices of required width from stalk to root end. See diagram below step 8.

Keep slices in bowl of very cold water until required. Drain before use.

How to blanch

Blanching is a process which does one of three things:

(a) removes skins
(b) whitens foods
(c) kills enzymes prior to freezing.

To remove the skins from tomatoes, nuts, etc. or to prepare vegetables for freezing, plunge into boiling water.

To whiten veal or remove impurities and bitterness from pickled beef, place in cold water, bring to boil and skim whilst hot.

The exception to using water for blanching is when blanching chipped potatoes. These should be plunged into very hot oil for a few moments. They can then be placed on one side for use later in the day or stored in the freezer until required.

How to skin tomatoes

1 Immerse tomatoes in boiling water for 20 sec.
2 Remove with spoon and dip into cold water.
3 The skins will then split or wrinkle and pull off easily.

Buy tomatoes when they are underripe and leave near a window to ripen. Overripe tomatoes are usually half price and are very good for cooking. They should not be skinned before using or they will become too soft to handle. If there is a visible green spot at the stalk end, it indicates that the tomato is going bad. Canned tomatoes are good value. Use them in soups, stews, sauces or in vegetable dishes such as ratatouille. The liquor should not be discarded.

How to make pastry using PU margarine

1 Place PU margarine in coldest part of refrigerator or freezer until firm.

2 Chill mixing bowl if possible.
3 Sieve flour and salt together into a mixing bowl.
4 Add PU margarine to flour and cut with a knife until pieces of fat are very small and each is coated with flour.
5 Rinse hands under cold water and dry well.
6 Rub PU margarine into flour with finger tips until mixture resembles bread crumbs.
7 Add cold water or preferably cold skimmed milk all at once.
8 Mix with knife to form a dough, then gently knead with the fingers.

One teaspoonful of water or milk *must* be allowed to each ounce of flour. More may be added if the mixture will not bind. If the paste is sticky when only the minimum amount of liquid is used, lightly flour and place covered in the refrigerator for at least 30 min. Should the paste remain difficult to handle, place on a sheet of greaseproof paper or vegetable parchment. Cover with another sheet of paper and roll out over the top of this. Remove the top sheet of paper and using the bottom piece as a guide invert onto a pie dish.

How to make pastry using PU oil
Less oil per ounce is needed. Use 1 oz. PU oil to 3 oz. flour. 2 tbsps. PU oil = 1 oz. Allow approximately 1 tbsp. water to 3 oz. flour.

1 Sieve the flour and salt into a mixing bowl.
2 Sprinkle oil over the surface with a fork.
3 Mix with a knife until the mixture resembles breadcrumbs.
4 Add sufficient water or skimmed milk to form a stiff dough.

Use as required.
Ingredients and utensils may be at room temperature. Pastry made with PU oil is very good but not as 'short' as that made with PU margarine.

How to bake blind
(*A*)
1 Tear a piece of greaseproof paper to cover the inside base and sides of a pastry case.

2 Grease the paper and press the greased side against the pastry.
3 Fill with uncooked rice, lentils or dried beans.
4 Bake in a preheated oven 400 or 6 for 10 min.
5 Grasp the edges of the paper with both hands and remove, making sure that the beans do not fall and stick to the pastry.
6 Unless the case is to be filled and cooked, switch off the gas or electricity and return the pastry to the oven to dry.

Baking 'beans' should be stored in a screwtop jar and may be used time and time again.

(B)
1 Crumple a large piece of aluminium foil to fill the pastry case.
2 Grease the side of the foil that touches the pastry.
3 Bake 400 or 6 as above.

How to line a flan ring

1 Roll out pastry to a round.
2 To determine the correct size, hold the flan ring over the pastry and turn the ring upright onto its side. Mark the outer edge with the handle of a spoon. Repeat at six points round a rough circle.
3 Remove flan ring and cut pastry through the marked points to make the flan ring circle. Flan rings are usually 1 in. deep; therefore a 6 in. ring will require pastry 8 in. in diameter.
4 Grease an upturned baking sheet and stand flan ring in centre.
5 Flour the pastry and fold into four.

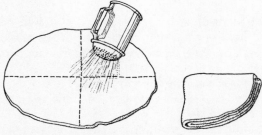

Lining a flan ring—fold into four

6 Place the pointed end of the pastry on the baking sheet in the centre of the flan ring and unfold evenly.

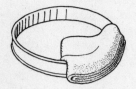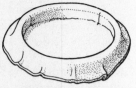

Lining a flan ring—unfold evenly

7 Form some of the pastry trimmings into a ball and use this to press the dough into the base of the ring. Do not stretch the pastry, but push it gently into the tin from the edges.
8 Roll a rolling pin over top of tin to remove any surplus pastry.
9 Using both thumbs, press up the pastry around the sides of the tin, so that pastry protrudes about $\frac{1}{4}$ in.
10 If baking blind, prick the base with a fork.

When the pastry is cooked, lift off the flan ring with oven gloves.

How to line a tin

Round Tins
1 Grease the inside of the tin.
2 Stand the tin on a piece of greaseproof paper.
3 Draw a line on the paper round the outside of the base of the tin.
4 Remove the tin and cut out the circle of paper inside the pencil line.
5 Cut a further piece of greaseproof paper. This will be the length of the tin's circumference by the depth of the tin plus 1 in. You will then have a long rectangular piece of paper.
6 Fold up 1 in. along the length of this strip.
7 Unfold again and at $1\frac{1}{2}$ in. intervals make cuts as far as the crease in the 1 in. fold.
8 Fit this strip inside the tin with the cut edges overlapping in the base.

9 Place the round piece of paper over, to cover.
10 Grease the whole.

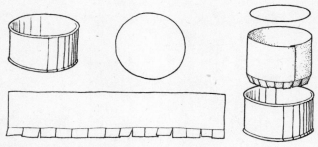

Lining a round tin

Square or oblong tins
1 Grease the inside of the tin.
2 Stand the tin on a large piece of greaseproof paper and draw line on paper round base of tin.
3 Remove the tin and measure depth.
4 Add this measurement all round line previously drawn on paper and cut.
5 Turn greaseproof paper over.
6 Fold along lines of original base.
7 Open out and make cuts in alternate folds from edges of paper to pencil line.
8 Turn up sides to form a box shape with the cut ends overlapping in the same direction to prevent leakages.
9 Fit into tin and press against sides and base.
10 Grease the lining paper.

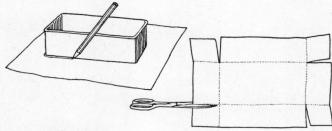

Lining an oblong tin

If the tin has sloping sides, follow the above instructions to step 6 and then open out the paper and cut from the points diagonally to the right-angled corners of the pencilled base.

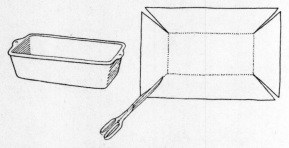

Lining a tin with sloping sides

How to 'flambé'
This is the french term meaning 'to flame'.
1 Pour brandy, wine or liqueur over food in pan.
2 Bring to the boil and ignite the liquid with a match.
3 Switch off heat and shake pan until flames die down.

The purpose of flambé is to remove the pure alcohol and impregnate the food with the flavour of the liqueur or wine chosen. Sometimes the flames leap quite high, but die down quickly. It is best to flambé with a lighted taper or a match gripped firmly with a pair of kitchen tongs.

Flambé

How to use a blender or liquidizer

A blender or liquidizer is a plastic or glass goblet which fits on to an electric mixer. It is also obtainable as an independent electric appliance. There is a revolving cutting blade that breaks the food into small particles. Its uses include making purée for soups, blending lumpy sauces, making breadcrumbs and grinding coffee beans.

A liquidizer operates best with small quantities. Do not fill the goblet more than one third when grinding dry ingredients. Assemble the liquidizer and remove the centre cap from the lid. Switch the machine to maximum, and gradually add the dry foods. Cover the opening with the palm of your hand. Use this method for chopping nuts and parsley, grinding sugar and coffee and making breadcrumbs. The goblet may be three quarters filled for blending a mixture of liquids and solids. The lid and centre cap should be closed securely, and a medium speed should probably be sufficient. Use for soups, sauces, hot and cold drinks and reconstituting dried skimmed milk. 2 oz. or 4½ heaped tbsps. of powdered milk placed in the goblet with 1 pint of cold water will produce one very smooth pint of milk. If the liquidizer is small, blend the powder with a little of the water, empty into a jug and stir in the remainder of the of the water.

The motor should not be run for more than 3 min. continuously but may be used again after a short interval. After use dismantle, rinse all parts in cold or warm water, dry well and loosely reassemble to allow air to circulate.

How to press through a sieve

1 Pour food mixture into a sieve or gravy strainer resting on a saucepan.
2 If liquid is not to be retained, throw it away before pressing food through the strainer. If you are keeping liquid make sure the saucepan is of large enough capacity.
3 Place the saucepan on a firm surface, and hold the handle of the sieve securely with one hand.
4 Draw the back of a wooden spoon over the entire surface of the sieve and press well.
5 Lift up sieve and scrape pulp from underside into saucepan with a metal spoon or palette knife.

6 Continue pressing and scraping until all the food is passed through.

Fibrous matter, bay leaves, tomato skins etc. will remain in the strainer and should be discarded.

How to make a basic white sauce

A white sauce is a combination of fat, flour and milk in specific proportions, cooked in a saucepan over gentle heat until the mixture thickens. There are two methods generally employed.

(*A*)

Melt the fat in the saucepan, stir in the flour and cook for one minute.

Gradually add the milk and stir constantly over low heat until the mixture thickens and boils. Cook for 2 mins. Add salt and pepper

(*B*)

Place fat, flour and milk together in saucepan. Stir. Place over gentle heat and whisk until mixture thickens. Cook 2 mins. Add salt and pepper.

Always use equal quantities of fat and flour

Proportions for 1 *pint sauce*

1 oz. PU margarine or butter 1 oz. white flour 1 pint skimmed or whole milk	Thin or pouring sauce
2 oz. PU margarine or butter 2 oz. white flour 1 pint skimmed or whole milk	Medium thick or coating sauce
4 oz. PU margarine or butter 4 oz. white flour 1 pint skimmed or whole milk	Binding sauce or panada

A coating sauce should adhere to the back of a spoon.
A binding sauce should leave the sides of the saucepan and form a sticky ball.

How to warm syrup or jam

1 Place syrup or jam in a heatproof bowl.
2 One third fill a saucepan with hot water.
3 Place saucepan over low heat and either rest bowl on rim or crumple a piece of aluminium foil in the bottom of the saucepan and stand the bowl in the water. The water must not reach more than halfway up the sides of the bowl.
4 Bring the water slowly to the boil and switch off heat. The syrup should now be warm and liquid.

If using the second method in step three make sure no water bubbles over into the syrup.

Butter, sugar etc. may be melted simultaneously.

When making a glaze: jam and water are mixed directly in the saucepan and brought to the boil slowly to reduce.

Yeast

Yeast is a living organism of the fungi family. It is very sensitive to heat and humidity and must have suitable conditions in which to grow. Yeast must be dissolved in liquid at blood temperature. This should feel neither hot nor cold to the touch. Both salt and sugar are essential in yeast cookery but an excess will kill the yeast cells. Salt gives flavour, strengthens the protein in the flour and helps to create a larger volume in a finished loaf. If too little is used, the dough will be sticky and unmanageable. The correct proportions are $\frac{1}{4}$ oz. salt to 1 lb. flour. Sugar is food for the yeast, but as there is already a little sugar in flour, there is no necessity to cream the yeast and sugar. In fact this additional mixing would weaken the action of the yeast. In cooking, the yeast gives off carbon dioxide which creates the open texture in cooked yeast mixtures.

Yeast is sometimes obtainable at delicatessen shops and bakers, and will keep for a few days in a loosely tied polythene bag on the lowest shelf of the refrigerator. Yeast darkens as it goes stale. Dried yeast, sold in most grocers and supermarkets, should not be kept too long after opening. Use half the quantity of dried yeast to fresh yeast given in a recipe, and dissolve in the liquid but leave about 10 min. before adding to the flour.

Yeast is a valuable source of Vitamin B.

Rising and Proving yeast dough

1 Add yeast liquid to flour and salt as directed in the recipe.
2 Work with hand or electric dough hook until mixture is elastic and tends to leave side of bowl. It is better to have the dough too wet rather than too dry. More flour may be added when knocking back.
3 Cover the dough with a damp cloth or self-adhering plastic film, or place in a greased polythene bag knotted well above mixture.
4 Leave in a warm but not hot place to rise until dough is double its original size. The bubbles will now be clearly visible and the dough will have a 'bath sponge' texture.
5 Turn onto floured board and knock back. This means punching the dough so that the carbon dioxide bubbles are spread evenly through the mixture.
6 Shape and cover with greased polythene or paper.
7 Leave to prove 15 min. until dough regains its shape. To test, press on dough with finger tips. The imprint should disappear immediately and the dough spring back into shape.
8 Bake in a hot, pre-heated oven.

Appendix one
Weights and measures

A miscellany of useful items of information

1 teacup holds 6 fl. oz. liquid

8 tbsps. = 5 fl. oz.	= ¼ pint
1 tbsp. oil	= ½ fl. oz.
1 teacup breakfast cereal	= 1 oz.
2 level tbsps. ground nuts	= 1 oz.
1 level tbsp. rice	= 1 oz.
2 level tbsps. flour	= 1 oz.
1 level tbsp. caster sugar	= 1 oz.
5 level tbsps. breadcrumbs	= 1 oz.
1 level tbsp. grated cheese	= ¼ oz.
3 level tbsps. icing sugar	= 1 oz.
1 level tbsp. warm golden syrup	= 1 oz.
1 level tbsp. cold golden syrup	= 2 oz.
2 level tbsps. currants, raisins or sultanas	= 1 oz.
2 level tbsps. cocoa powder	= 1 oz.
Juice of 1 lemon	= 3 tbsps. approx.

A pinch is the amount that can be held between the thumb and forefinger

In the recipes, unless stated, a tbsp. means a level tablespoonful and a tsp. means a level teaspoonful.

Sets of British Standard measuring spoons can be purchased in plastic or metal.

To measure a level spoonful, draw a knife across the edges of the spoon to remove surplus ingredients.

Where weights are given, it is preferable to use scales

rather than guess, but the items mentioned above will provide quick approximate measures.

20 fl. oz.	= 1 pint
4 gills	= 1 pint
1 gill	= $\frac{1}{4}$ pint

1 large egg weighs $2\frac{3}{8}$ oz. with shell
1 standard egg weighs 2 oz. with shell
1 medium egg weighs $1\frac{3}{4}$ oz. with shell

Metric conversions
Lengths are to be measured in
    millimetres (one thousandth of a metre)   mm.
    centimetres (one hundreth of a metre)   cm.
Areas are to be measured in square centimetres cm.^{2}
Volumes are to be measured in cubic centimetres cm.^{3}
Capacity is to be measured in
    millilitres (one thousandth of a litre)   ml.
    centilitres (one hundreth of a litre)   cl.
    decilitres (one tenth of a litre)   dl.
    litres   l.
Weight is to be measured in
    grammes (one thousandth of a kilogramme)   gm.
    kilogrammes   kg.

1 oz.	=	28.35 gm.
2 oz.	=	56.7 gm.
4 oz.	=	113.4 gm.
8 oz.	=	226.8 gm.
12 oz.	=	340.2 gm.
16 oz.	=	453.6 gm.
1 kg.	=	2.2 lb.

But for normal cooking conversion purposes, 1 oz. can be said to equal 30 gm., and 100 gm. approximately $3\frac{1}{2}$ oz.

$\frac{1}{4}$ pint	= 142 ml.
$\frac{1}{2}$ pint	= 284 ml.
1 pint	= 568 ml.
$\frac{1}{2}$ l.	= 0·88 pint
1 l.	= 1.76 pints (i.e. 1 litre = approx. $1\frac{3}{4}$ pints)

1 in.   = 2.54 cm
6 in.   = 15.2 cm
39.37 in. = 1 metre = 100 cm.

Refrigerator temperatures

The temperature within the refrigerator will naturally depend on whether the control is at 'low' or 'high'. The range will normally give a variation between 40 and 47°F.

The frozen storage compartments are marked on the door with asterisks to indicate their capabilities.

*	21°F. keeps ready frozen foods for 1 week
**	10°F. keeps ready frozen foods for 1 month
***	0°F. keeps ready frozen foods for 3 months
****	0—−10°F. freezes and stores fresh foods and stores frozen foods up to 12 months

Fahrenheit	Celsius
21°	−6°
10°	−12°
0°	−18°
−10°	−23°

Approximate equivalent oven temperatures

Gas	Electric Fahrenheit	Electric Celsius	
$\frac{1}{4}$	225	110	⎫
$\frac{1}{2}$	250	120	⎬ Very cool
1	275	135	⎭
2	300	150	Cool
3	325	165	Warm
4	350	180	⎫ Moderate
5	375	190	⎭
6	400	200	Fairly hot
7	425	220	Hot
8	450	230	⎫ Very hot
9	475	240	⎭

The temperatures given in the recipes are all measured in Fahrenheit.

Appendix two
Tables referred to in text

Table 2
Calorific values

Approximate calories in everyday foods in the normal diet

Item	Unit	Value	Average helping	
BISCUITS, BREAD AND CEREALS				
Biscuits	values usually printed on the packet			
commercial				
dry crackers			1 biscuit	28
semi-sweet			1 biscuit	35
filled sweet			1 biscuit	70
digestive			1 biscuit	74
Bread			1 thin slice	55
Breadcrumbs	1 oz.	97		
Cornflakes	1 oz.	100	2 tbsps.	50
Flour	1 oz.	99	4 oz.	396
Macaroni, cooked	1 oz.	38	2 oz.	76
Rice, cooked	1 oz.	35	2 oz.	70
Spaghetti, cooked	1 oz.	31	3 oz.	93

Item	Unit	Value	Average helping	
CHEESES, MILKS, ETC.				
Milk				
whole	1 oz.	20	1 pint	400
skimmed	1 oz.	11	1 pint	220
non-fat dried				
(reconstituted)	1 oz.	11	1 pint	220
Buttermilk				
(made from				
skimmed milk)	1 oz.	11	¼ pint	55
Powdered coffee				
creamers	1 level tsp.	11	¼ pint	11
Cream				
single	1 oz.	62	1 tbsp.	40
double	1 oz.	131	1 tbsp.	80
Cheese				
camembert	1 oz.	86	1¼ oz. wedge	108
cheddar	1 oz.	115	1 in. cube	70
cottage	1 oz.	30	2 oz.	60
danish blue	1 oz.	103	1 oz.	103
edam	1 oz.	88	1½ oz.	132
parmesan	1 oz.	130	1 tbsp.	25
processed	1 oz.	106	1 oz.	106
Yoghurt				
natural low fat	5 oz.	90	1 carton	90
fruit low fat	6 oz.	162	1 carton	162
Eggs				
1 large raw egg	$2\frac{3}{16}$ oz.	80	1 egg	80
1 egg white	$1\frac{3}{16}$ oz.	15		
1 egg yolk	1 oz.	65		
FATS AND OILS				
Butter	1 oz.	226	¼ oz. (1 wrapped portion)	56
French dressing	1 oz.	114	2 tbsps.	114
Lard	1 oz.	263		
Margarine				
hard	1 oz.	226		
PU	1 oz.	205		
Mayonnaise	1 oz.	200	1 tbsp.	100

Item	Unit	Value	Average helping	
Oil				
corn	1 oz.	252	1 tbsp.	125
cottonseed	1 oz.	252	1 tbsp.	125
olive	1 oz.	252	1 tbsp.	125
peanut	1 oz.	252	1 tbsp.	125
safflower	1 oz.	252	1 tbsp.	125
soybean	1 oz.	252	1 tbsp.	125
Vegetable fats	1 oz.	251		
White sauce	1 oz.	45	1 tbsp.	45
FISH				
Cod				
boiled	1 oz.	19	1 medium steak	110
fried	1 oz.	36	1 medium steak	180
Haddock				
fried	1 oz.	46	4 oz.	184
poached	1 oz.	21	4 oz.	84
smoked	1 oz.	18	1 fillet	100
Kipper, grilled	1 oz.	31	1 pair	200
Salmon				
fresh	1 oz.	46	4 oz.	184
canned	1 oz.	39	2 tbsps.	140
Sole, grilled	1 oz.	18	1 medium	100
Tuna, canned in oil	1 oz.	57	2 oz.	114
FRUIT				
Apples				
eating	1 oz.	10	1 average	30
cooking	1 oz.	10	4 oz. sweet-ened cooked	80
Apricots				
dried	1 oz.	52	2 oz. stewed	104
fresh	1 oz.	7	4 oz.	28
Avocados	half	100	half	100
Bananas	1 oz.	22	1 medium	50
Blackberries	1 oz.	17	3 oz.	51
Cherries				
canned	1 oz.	20	3 tbsps.	120
fresh	1 oz.	11	12 cherries	30

Item	Unit	Value	Average helping	
Dates	1 oz. pitted	80	6 dates	80
Figs, dried	1 oz.	75	1 fig	60
Fruit salad, canned	1 oz.	24	2 tbsps.	48
Gooseberries				
canned	1 oz.	12	3 tbsps.	80
fresh	1 oz.	10	8 medium	40
Grapes	1 oz.	17	12 grapes	34
Grapefruit fresh	1 oz.	3	½ fruit	20
Lemons	1 lemon	20	1 teacup fruit juice	40
Melon	1 oz.	5	½ melon	40
Oranges	1 oz.	8	1 average	40
fresh juice (canned)			1 teacupful	70
Peaches, fresh	1 oz.	9	1 average	40
Pears, fresh	1 oz.	9	1 average	80
Pineapple				
canned	1 oz.	18	3 tbsps.	100
fresh	1 oz.	13	1 slice	50
juice canned	1 oz.	17	1 teacupful	85
Plums, fresh	1 oz.	14	2 plums	30
Prunes, dried	1 oz.	70	4 prunes	70
Raisins, seedless	1 oz.	80	1 oz.	80
Raspberries	1 oz.	18	3 tbsps.	50
Rhubarb	negligible			
Strawberries, fresh	1 oz.	7	6 large	20

MEAT AND POULTRY

Item	Unit	Value	Average helping	
Bacon	1 oz.	169	3 rashers	340
Beef				
corned	1 oz.	66	3 oz.	198
lean braised	1 oz.	56	3 oz.	168
lean minced grilled	1 oz.	62	3 oz.	186
lean grilled steak	1 oz.	58	1 6 oz. steak	342
Chicken				
boiled	1 oz.	38	4 slices	200
roast	1 oz.	29	4 slices	150
Lamb				
5 oz. grilled chop, lean only	2½ oz.	140	2 'eyes'	280
roast leg lean	1 oz.	53	3 oz.	159
Liver	1 oz.	74	2 slices	250

Item	Unit	Value	Average helping	
Pork				
3½ oz. grilled chop, lean only	1⅔ oz.	130	2 'eyes'	260
roast, lean only	1 oz.	70	3 oz.	210
Veal				
grilled cutlet	1 oz.	62	1 3 oz. cutlet	186
roast	1 oz.	77	3 oz.	231
NUTS				
Almonds				
shelled	1 oz.	170		
ground	1 oz.	170		
Peanuts, roast and salted	1 oz.	168		
Walnuts	1 oz.	176		
SUNDRIES				
Chocolate milk and plain	1 oz.	160		
Marshmallows	1 oz.	90		
Honey	1 oz.	88	1 tbsp.	21
Jam	1 oz.	77	1 tbsp.	20
Sugar	1 oz.	112	1 tsp.	30
VEGETABLES				
Asparagus	4 spears	10	8 spears	20
Bean shoots	1 oz.	8	3 oz.	24
Beans, green	1 oz.	7	3 tbsps.	21
Beetroot	1 oz.	13	small beetroot	30
Broccoli	1 oz.	8	4 oz.	32
Brussels sprouts	1 oz.	11	8 sprouts	55
Cabbage				
cooked	1 oz.	6	4 oz.	24
raw	1 oz.	7	2 oz.	14
Carrots	1 oz.	9	3 oz.	27
Cauliflower	1 oz.	6	3 oz.	18
Celery	1 oz.	4	2 stalks	10
Corn, sweet	1 cob	70	1 cob	70
Cucumber	1 medium	30	6 slices	3
Lettuce	1 average	30	a few leaves	3
Mushrooms	1 oz.	5	4 or 5 mushrooms	5

Item	Unit	Value	Average helping	
Onions	1 oz.	10	2 oz.	20
Parsnips	1 oz.	16	3 tbsps.	50
Peas, cooked	1 oz.	20	3 tbsps.	80
Peppers, green	1 oz.	6	1 whole cooked	15
Potatoes				
boiled	1 oz.	23	2 small	100
chipped	1 oz.	68	2 tbsps.	300
roast	1 oz.	35	2 small	140
Radishes	4	5	4	5
Spinach	1 oz.	6	3 oz.	18
Tomatoes,				
fresh	1 oz.	5	1 average	10
canned	1 8 oz. can	50	2 oz.	12
Turnips	1 oz	6	2 oz.	12

WINES AND SPIRITS AND OTHER DRINKS

	Unit	Value	Average helping	
Beer	1 fl. oz.	10	½ pint	100
Gin	1 fl. oz.	70	1 double	105
Rum	1 fl. oz.	70	1 double	105
Vodka	1 fl. oz.	70	1 double	105
Whisky	1 fl. oz.	70	1 double	105
Cider	1 fl. oz.	12	½ pint	120
Cola type	1 fl. oz.	12	tumbler	60
Sherry	1 fl. oz.	38	glass	80
Table wine	1 fl. oz.	20–26	glass	100–130
Soda water	1 fl. oz.	9	tumbler	45

NOTE. Do not forget that cooking additives such as sugar and margarine will increase the calorific content of the above basic values.

Table 3
Fatty acid content of foods

Item	Amount in edible portion of 100 grams		
	Total saturated fatty acids (gm.)	Unsaturated fatty acids oleic (gm.)	linoleic (gm.)
BREAD, BISCUITS AND CAKES			
Biscuits			
cheese	8	10	1
chocolate digestive	7	15	1
sweet	3	8	1
Bread, white	1	2	trace
Doughnuts	6	17	2
Rolls	1	3	1
FATS, MILK EXTRACTS AND OILS			
Butter	46	27	2
Cheese			
cheddar	18	11	1
cottage	2	1	trace
cream	21	12	1
soufflé	9	6	1
Cream			
double	21	12	1
single	17	10	1
Fats, cooking			
animal	43	41	11
vegetable	23	65	7
Lard	38	46	10
Margarine			
hydrogenated	18	47	14
PU	19	31	29
Milk			
canned evaporated	4	3	trace
partially skimmed	1	1	trace
whole	2	1	trace
Oil			
corn	10	28	53
cottonseed	22	21	49
olive	11	76	7
safflower	8	15	72

Item	Total saturated fatty acids (gm.)	Unsaturated fatty acids oleic (gm.)	linoleic (gm.)
soya bean	15	20	52
Peanut butter	9	25	14
FISH			
Herrings	2	1	2
Salmon	5	5	trace
pink, canned	2	1	trace
Trout	3	2	trace
Tuna	3	2	2
FRUIT AND VEGETABLES			
Avocados	3	7	2
Chick peas	Trace	2	2
Peppers	3	2	trace
MEATS			
Bacon, sliced	22	33	6
Chop suey, canned	1	1	trace
Corned beef	15	13	1
Ham	10	11	2
Hamburger	10	9	trace
Lamb	12	8	1
Liver	1	1	trace
Luncheon meat	6	7	2
Pork	10	11	2
sausage	18	21	5
Rabbit	3	3	1
Steak			
chuck	15	14	1
porterhouse	17	16	1
rump	12	11	1
Veal	6	5	trace
Venison	3	1	trace
NUTS			
Almonds	4	36	11
Brazils	13	32	17
Coconuts	30	2	trace
Cashews	8	32	3
Hazelnuts	3	34	10

Item	Total saturated fatty acids (gm.)	Unsaturated fatty acids oleic (gm.)	linoleic (gm.)
Peanuts	10	20	14
Pistachio	5	35	10
Walnuts	4	10	40
POULTRY			
Chicken, fried			
(flesh and skin)	3	6	2
(dark meat with skin)	4	6	2
(dark meat no skin)	3	4	1
Chow mein (chicken)	1	1	1
Turkey			
total edible	4	6	3
flesh only	2	3	1
skin only	11	17	8
SUNDRIES			
Chocolate			
bitter or cooking	30	20	1
drinking	1	1	trace
Cocoa powder	1	1	trace
Coleslaw with mayonnaise	2	3	7
Custard, baked	3	2	trace
Eggs			
whole	4	5	1
yolks	10	13	2
fried	6	7	1
Noodles	1	2	trace
Salad dressing, french (made with corn oil)	7	20	37
Soya flour	3	4	11
Wheat germ	2	2	4
breakfast cereals (commercial)	2	3	6

NOTE. 100 gm. = 3½ oz. approx.

Table 4

Comparison of saturated and unsaturated fatty acids in oils and fats

Food	Linoleic acid (PU) %	Oleic acid (Mono-unsaturated) %	Saturated fatty acids %
Safflower oil	76	15	8
Sunflower oil	66	21	12
Corn oil	55	30	12
Cottonseed oil	51	22	26
Peanut oil	31	50	19
Olive oil	8	80	12
Butter	3	35	59
Lard	11	48	40

Adapted from Callie M. Coon's *Fatty Acids in Some Animal and Plant Foods.*

Table 5
Heights and Weights

Age next birth-day	ft. 5 in. 3 st. lb.	ft. 5 in. 4 st. lb.	ft. 5 in. 5 st. lb.	ft. 5 in. 6 st. lb.	ft. 5 in. 7 st. lb.	ft. 5 in. 8 st. lb.	ft. 5 in. 9 st. lb.	ft. 5 in. 10 st. lb.	ft. 5 in. 11 st. lb.	ft. 6 in. 0 st. lb.	ft. 6 in. 1 st. lb.	ft. 6 in. 2 st. lb.	ft. 6 in. 3 st. lb.
18	8 9	8 12	9 1	9 5	9 8	9 12	10 2	10 6	10 10	11 0	11 5	11 10	12 1
19	8 10	8 13	9 2	9 6	9 9	10 0	10 4	10 8	10 12	11 2	11 7	11 12	12 3
20	8 11	9 0	9 4	9 7	9 11	10 1	10 5	10 9	10 13	11 3	11 8	11 13	12 4
21	8 12	9 1	9 6	9 9	9 12	10 2	10 6	10 11	11 1	11 5	11 10	12 1	12 6
22	8 13	9 2	9 7	9 10	9 13	10 4	10 8	10 13	11 2	11 6	11 11	12 2	12 7
23	9 0	9 3	9 8	9 11	10 0	10 5	10 9	11 0	11 4	11 8	11 13	12 4	12 9
24	9 1	9 4	9 10	9 12	10 1	10 5	10 10	11 1	11 5	11 9	12 0	12 5	12 10
25	9 2	9 5	9 11	9 12	10 2	10 7	10 11	11 2	11 6	11 10	12 1	12 7	12 12
26	9 3	9 6	9 12	9 13	10 3	10 8	10 12	11 3	11 7	11 11	12 3	12 8	13 0
27	9 3	9 7	9 13	10 0	10 3	10 9	10 13	11 4	11 8	11 13	12 4	12 10	13 2
28	9 4	9 8	10 0	10 1	10 4	10 10	11 0	11 5	11 9	12 0	12 5	12 12	13 3
29	9 4	9 9	10 1	10 1	10 5	10 11	11 1	11 6	11 10	12 1	12 6	12 12	13 4
30	9 5	9 10	10 2	10 2	10 6	10 12	11 2	11 6	11 11	12 2	12 8	13 0	13 6
31	9 6	9 11	10 3	10 3	10 6	10 13	11 3	11 7	11 12	12 2	12 9	13 1	13 7
32	9 6	9 12	10 4	10 4	10 7	11 0	11 4	11 8	11 13	12 3	12 10	13 2	13 8
33	9 7	9 13	10 5	10 5	10 8	11 1	11 5	11 9	12 0	12 4	12 11	13 3	13 9
34	9 8	10 0	10 6	10 6	10 9	11 2	11 5	11 10	12 1	12 5	12 13	13 4	13 10
35	9 8	10 1	10 7	10 6	10 10	11 0	11 6	11 10	12 1	12 6	13 0	13 5	13 11
36	9 9	10 2	10 8	10 6	10 10	11 1	11 7	11 10	12 2	12 7	13 0	13 5	13 11

Age	1	2	3	4	5	6	7	8	9	10	11	12	13
37	9 8	9 12	10 2	10 6	10 11	11 1	11 6	11 11	12 2	12 7	13 1	13 6	13 12
38	9 9	9 13	10 3	10 7	10 12	11 2	11 7	11 12	12 3	12 8	13 2	13 7	13 13
39	9 9	10 0	10 3	10 7	10 12	11 2	11 7	11 12	12 3	12 8	13 2	13 8	14 0
40	9 10	10 0	10 4	10 8	10 13	11 3	11 8	11 13	12 4	12 9	13 3	13 9	14 1
41	9 11	10 1	10 5	10 9	11 0	11 3	11 9	12 0	12 5	12 9	13 3	13 10	14 2
42	9 11	10 1	10 5	10 9	11 0	11 4	11 9	12 0	12 5	12 10	13 4	13 11	14 2
43	9 12	10 2	10 6	10 10	11 1	11 5	11 10	12 1	12 6	12 11	13 5	13 11	14 3
44	9 12	10 2	10 6	10 11	11 1	11 6	11 11	12 1	12 6	12 12	13 6	13 12	14 3
45	9 13	10 3	10 7	10 11	11 2	11 6	11 11	12 2	12 7	12 12	13 6	13 12	14 4
46	10 0	10 3	10 8	10 12	11 3	11 7	11 12	12 3	12 8	12 13	13 7	13 13	14 4
47	10 0	10 4	10 8	10 13	11 3	11 8	11 13	12 3	12 8	13 0	13 8	14 0	14 5
48	10 1	10 5	10 9	11 0	11 4	11 8	12 0	12 4	12 9	13 1	13 8	14 1	14 6
49	10 1	10 5	10 9	11 0	11 5	11 9	12 0	12 5	12 9	13 1	13 9	14 1	14 6
50	10 2	10 6	10 10	11 1	11 5	11 9	12 1	12 5	12 10	13 2	13 10	14 2	14 7
51	10 2	10 6	10 10	11 1	11 6	11 10	12 1	12 6	12 10	13 2	13 10	14 2	14 8
52	10 3	10 7	10 11	11 2	11 6	11 11	12 2	12 6	12 11	13 3	13 11	14 3	14 8
53	10 3	10 7	10 11	11 2	11 7	11 11	12 2	12 7	12 11	13 3	13 11	14 3	14 9
54	10 4	10 8	10 12	11 3	11 8	11 12	12 3	12 7	12 12	13 4	13 12	14 4	14 9

NOTES. For practical purposes a reduction of 1 lb. per stone can be made for females.

These are average weights and a 10% tolerance either way would not be excessive, and even 20% above might not be considered too obese.

Desirable weight is dependent on many health factors and these are taken into account at medical examinations for life insurance policies. It is normal to increase weight over the years so in this chart recall your weight at, say, 21 and your present weight should show the same percentage difference to the average.

Table 6
Choice of foods

	Foods to use	Foods to avoid
MILK	Skimmed Non-fat dried Buttermilk (made from skimmed milk without added cream) Cottage cheese Cheese (made from skimmed milk) Low fat or fat free yoghurt	Whole Evaporated Condensed Canned cream Fresh cream Ice cream Sour cream Cream substitute Whole milk buttermilk Whole milk yoghurt Cheese (made from whole milk) Butter
EGGS	Egg whites	Egg yolks (3 per week permitted)
FATS AND OILS	PU margarine Corn oil Safflower oil Sunflower oil Peanut Butter	Hard Margarine Whipped up cooking fats Lard Chicken fat Coconut oil
MEAT, FISH AND POULTRY	Poultry Fish Lean ham Veal Beef Lamb Pork	Poultry skin Shellfish (2 oz. equals 1 egg yolk) Duck Goose Bacon Offal (2 oz. may be substituted for 1 egg yolk) Visible fats on meat Sausages Fish roes Tongue

VEGETABLES AND FRUIT	All vegetables	Olives
	Almonds	Avocados
	Brazils	Cashew nuts
	Walnuts	Coconuts
	Peanuts	
	Pecans	
	Pistachios	
	All fruits except olives and avocados	
	Pulses	
OTHER FOODS	Sugar	Fudge
	Marmalade	Chocolate
	Jams	Commercial biscuits
	Honey	Commercial cakes
	Jellies	Cake mixes
	Marshmallows	Canned soups
	Fruit drops	
	Pickles	
	Matzos	
	Water biscuits	
	Crisp breads	
	Melba toast	
	Pasta	
	Canned consommé	
	Gelatine	

NOTE. In certain cases there may be variations of the 'foods to use' in the diet, on medical grounds.

Table 7
Yield of cooked meat per lb. of raw meat

Meat	Food as served	Weight after cooking
CHOPS, STEAK FOR GRILLING OR FRYING		
With bone and much fat (e.g. pork or lamb chops, beef rib, sirloin or porterhouse)	Lean, bone and fat	10–12 oz.
	Lean and fat	7–10 oz.
	Lean only	5–7 oz.
Without bone and with very little fat (e.g. top rump, veal)	Lean and fat	12–13 oz.
	Lean only	9–12 oz.
MINCE	Patties	9–13 oz.
ROASTS		
With fat (e.g. rib, loin, chuck, shoulder of lamb, leg of pork)	Lean, bone and fat	10–12 oz.
	Lean and fat	8–10 oz.
	Lean only	6–9 oz.
POT ROAST, SIMMERING, BRAISING, STEWING		
With bone and fat (e.g. chuck, pork shoulder)	Lean, bone and fat	10–11 oz.
	Lean and fat	8–9 oz.
	Lean only	6–8 oz.
Without bone, little fat (e.g. trimmed beef, veal)	Lean with adhering fat only	9–11 oz.

Appendix three
Bibliography

Ruth Bennett White   *Food and Your Future*
Corinne H Robinson   *Basic Nutrition and Diet Therapy*
Marjorie C Zukel   *Revising Booklets on Fat-Controlled Meals*
Callie M Coons   *Fatty Acids in Some Animals and Plant Foods*
Lawrence E Lamb   *Your Heart and How to Live with it*
American Heart Association   *Planning Fat-controlled meals*
US Department of Agriculture   *Handbook No. 8*
Van den Berghs and Jurgens Ltd   *What you should know about dietary fats and your health*
American Dietetic Association   *Cholesterol Content of Food*
Dorothea Turner   *Handbook of Diet Therapy*
Bernice K Watt and Annabel L Merrill   *Composition of Foods*
R P Cook   *Cholesterol*

Index